Praise for Making Friends

‘This book is an important r
the power to effect positive
body’

David R. Hamliton Ph.D Author of How Your Mind Can Heal Your Body

‘In this wonderful book Sarah Presley explains with searing honesty the journey that took her from debilitating illness to running a highly successful holistic business. She tells us about the profound difference mindfulness meditation has made to her life and gives us a roadmap to discovering what it can do for us. Sarah explains how meditation can change your life for the better. I wholeheartedly recommend this book to you.’

Mary Pearson, co-founder of the British School of Meditation and author of Meditation, the stress solution

‘Sarah's powerful, transformational story blended with years of experience & professional training are brought together in this wonderful book. It’s packed full of useful, accessible tools and insight around meditation and so much more. I really recommend it. Sarah’s work is a gift.’

Kim Ingleyby, Award Winning Coach, Tedx Speaker, Charity Adventurer, Author, Founder Energised Performance

'An incredible and very relatable book in which Sarah not only shares her personal journey of healing, but provides helpful, accessible advice and information on meditation. Her warmth, compassion and expertise shines through in her words and meditations, and you can tell she really cares about you as the reader as she guides you though your own journey within the book. I would highly recommend'

Catherine Banks, co-owner of the British School of Meditation

'Brilliant! Why meditate? This book will encourage you to give it a try or learn more about the ancient yet modern practice of meditation. Sarah's account of why she meditates is incredibly moving and the book offers inspiring and practical guidance of how to meditate yourself. It's a must read. I loved it!'

Catherine Thomlinson, co-owner of the British School of Meditation

Making Friends With Yourself

A Practical Guide on How Meditation Can Take You From Overwhelm to an Inner Calm

Published in the United Kingdom by:

Sealy Publishing
info@sealypublishing.co.uk

The information given in this book should not be treated as a substitute for professional medical advice; always consult a medical practitioner. Any use of information in this book is at the reader's discretion and risk. Neither the author nor the publisher can be held responsible for any loss, claim or damage arising out of the use, or misuse, of the suggestions made, the failure to take medical advice or for any material on third-party websites.

A catalogue record for this book is available from the British Library.

ISBN: 978-1-7393730-0-9

Table of Contents

Introduction

'I just want to lie and stare at the underside of the duvet'. My husband was trying to get me up to go to work and I didn't want to move. I had woken up feeling numb, but I knew if I removed the duvet everything would feel too much – too much noise, too many emotions, thoughts, deadlines, expectations, people . . . I felt I had given the world everything I could offer, and I had nothing left to give. I was overwhelmed and consumed by anxiety, fear and worry in every single minute of the day and didn't feel I could cope with even the basics of daily living. I was stripped of any fun, spontaneity, or fulfillment, and I could no longer access any joy. If I was completely honest, I just didn't like myself anymore.

My husband gave me a hug. 'Stay there,' he said. 'Don't fight the feeling or pretend to yourself this is all going to be OK. Allow yourself to be with this right now, and don't think about what happens tomorrow'.

Although we didn't know it at the time, my husband had delivered the basics of mindfulness – being present with where and who you are, with acceptance and without judgement.

Not long after this, I discovered a short chapter on meditation in a book about Buddhism, and the rest, as they say, is history. Through meditation I found a way to effect positive changes to my body and mind and take steps to make friends with myself again.

In the last few years, we have been living in extraordinary times. With the unexpected plot twist of COVID-19, and the continuing anxiety about climate change, war, and the cost of living crises, it can be hard not to be affected by it all. Taking care of yourself and your needs right now has never been more important, enabling you to feel more resilient, stronger, and healthier, and create more joy and satisfaction in your life.

*

Are you tired of feeling overwhelmed? The constant threat of emotions bubbling to the surface can be exhausting, impacting your personality and negatively affecting your relationships, health, home and work life. You may already feel like a shell of your former self, and all the coping strategies you used to use are no longer accessible to you. It may be difficult to concentrate or perform the simplest of tasks.

Do you want to find the tools to put your mind and body back into balance and rediscover yourself again, so you can live a life where you can flow with the ups and downs rather than fight, run away or feel overwhelmed by life's changes?

In this book, you will learn how mindfulness meditation can help you go from overwhelm to a calmer mindset, and how to establish the best foundations for your practice. You will also discover why you feel anxiety, worry and anger, and experience the inner critic and the pain of rejection, while exploring different meditation types and techniques to help you ride through these moments. In learning meditation, you can rediscover the best parts of yourself again.

For years, many people have dismissed meditation as 'woo' or pseudo-science, yet you will also find out about the research which proves meditation has both physiological and psychological benefits. Mindfulness meditation can support you to shift your perspective, helping you to discover the joy of moment-to-moment living and connect to a sense of inner peace.

I understand what it feels like to be overwhelmed. In my case, it led me to being diagnosed with a chronic condition at the age of twenty-six. During the five years that followed, I explored complementary therapies and discovered meditation. This is the book I wished I had read at that time. It would have helped me to understand why I felt like I did, and it would have supported me in taking the right steps to balancing out my health and well-being – and this is why I have written it for you.

When I had recovered from my condition I set up a complementary health business to support others with their healing and personal development. In particular, I worked with those facing overwhelm, burnout and a loss of identity as they juggled the pressures of work and home, and I tailored my training to help empower them to reconnect with themselves – as well as with the joy of everyday living.

Now I am a co-owner and trainer with the British School of Meditation, and since 2015 I have supported those who wish to go out into their corner of the world, to make a difference and help improve the lives of others with the life-changing skills of meditation. In my teachings, I utilise everything I have learnt about going from illness to wellness, as well as everything I have learnt about teaching meditation.

My wish for you is that you take a step forward and understand that you do not need to live the rest of your life suffering with overwhelm. Right now, there is an opportunity for you to understand why you feel the way you do, and to know there is another path in which you can learn new tools to rediscover who you are underneath all of the stress and worry. This path will enable you to discover and grow, to connect with yourself, others, and nature, to live in balance and harmony, but most of all, to be a friend to yourself again.

Disclaimer: This book is not intended to be a substitute for professional medical or counselling advice. If you are concerned about your physical or mental health, or have already been diagnosed with a condition, please do seek the advice of your medical health professional prior to practicing any of the meditations.

Chapter One:

Why I Meditate

'Pah! You're twenty-six, you haven't got kids – what do you know about exhaustion?' exclaimed my GP. The year is 1999, Halley's Comet has just been visible with the naked eye, and we are counting down the days to a new century. In the media there is a lot of talk about Y2K and how all the computers may glitch. My body appeared to have its own glitch and I had just explained to my GP how exhausting and excruciatingly painful it had been to live my life, both physically and mentally, over the past three years. In response, she dismissed me from the surgery with a wave of her hand.

The eventual diagnosis of ME (a condition that causes severe tiredness and a range of other symptoms) the following year created mixed feelings: I was relieved to have been given a label for how I was feeling, but the reality was very hard to accept. To everyone who had known me, I appeared to be a shell of my former self: I was worn out, sad and scared. Depression and anxiety were by-products of the symptoms, and some days the fatigue was so severe I didn't have the energy to leave my bed. With no known cure, I had been told it was likely I would have this chronic condition for the rest of my life, and this knowledge was a bitter pill to swallow. Although I wasn't suicidal, I couldn't see the point of living nor could I recognise any joy in my life. I had been derailed from everything I knew, and my inner light had been switched off.

From a young age I was highly sensitive, acting like a sponge to all the emotions around me. If someone was sad, angry, or worried, I would absorb their feelings, not knowing how to let them go. I often felt I was living on the edge and began to worry excessively about everyone in my life. Eventually it developed into an anxious feeling which I would refer to as a 'a headache in my tummy' – I didn't know how else to describe the big bunched up ball of pain I carried around in my abdomen. An introverted and shy child, I would often hide behind my mother's legs if anyone looked at or spoke to me.

At primary school, absorbing emotions and being introverted meant I found friendships to be complicated and confusing. My parents' divorce brought relief to a tense home life, but it would be a year before I would tell any of my friends for fear of their rejection. Divorce is now commonplace, but when I was eight years old it seemed out of the ordinary. As I grew older, I found it easier to project a confident exterior to hide my sad and lonely feelings, and I also learnt to overcompensate for how I was feeling by becoming a people pleaser.

In secondary school, however, the strain of being a people pleaser began to take its toll. The social complexities of being a teenager meant one wrong step and you could be singled out by the bullies, and that was where I found myself in the build up to my exams. The death of a few friends also hit me hard at this time and I didn't know how to deal with the shock and sadness, so instead I ignored these emotions to bury the anger and trauma. To cope, I would lose myself in the music I listened to, and it was around this time I joined my first band as the lead singer. I also developed a love for acting – becoming another character in a play or in a band meant I didn't have to be me.

I thought I would be able to put the bullying behind me when I walked into my first job at the age of sixteen, but this time, I was singled out by an older woman for regular verbal abuse. Still eager to please, I would work extra hours rather than saying no, and I set the bar high for myself in the standard of work I would do. Desperate to catch up with the lives of my older sisters, I bought my first house at the age of eighteen – but not long after, financial pressures were added to the mix when a recession hit. In an attempt to fit in with social normalities, I married at the age of twenty-one, but was already divorced by the time I was twenty-four. The feeling of being a failure at marriage was immense and I worried I had let everyone down.

To the outside world I looked happy, outgoing, and confident. I was the epitome of the prominent 'work hard, play hard' nineties lifestyle, working my way up the career ladder in an assurance company and at the same time pursuing my dreams of being a singer in a punk rock band. The dreams even started to come to fruition: a top London modelling agency sponsored my band and as we began touring the UK we gained a little interest from the record industry. But the fatigue warning signs had been creeping in for a long time. Not knowing how to act upon them, I continued to ignore them instead.

I began to feel as if I was drowning in negative emotions, and I couldn't switch off from my constant destructive thoughts. I would overanalyse everything, and at the same time I was still putting all my energy into trying to keep everyone in my life happy. I spent most days fearful of when the black cloud of depression would descend, plus anxiety was still a daily passenger. All of this began to chip away at me and I started to feel so tired. Reading had always brought so much pleasure, but now I barely had the energy to hold a book in my hands – let alone concentrate on the words. As my exhaustion crept up, my life started crashing down around me. With my dreams rapidly falling apart, I was left wondering where it had all gone wrong.

It is no wonder my mind and body gave up. I had ignored and buried all the warning signs. Little did I know, at this point, that having ME was going to be the best thing to happen to me. It was going to give me the opportunity to be reborn, to start looking at life through a new lens and with a new and improved perspective. I was going to awaken, and I was going to heal. I was going to have a new appreciation for life.

But first, I was going to reach the lowest point of my life.

'I just don't see the point of life anymore'. I admitted to my mum a few weeks after the ME diagnosis. I had been desperate to know what was wrong with me, but the reality of living with fatigue and pain for the rest of my life made for a bleak future. I could see the fear in my mum's eyes as she sharply sucked in her breath. She thought she was going to lose me forever.

What took place next would be something I would replay in my head for many years after. As Mum sucked in her breath, I felt myself floating out of my body and floating into her body. I found myself looking at me through her eyes and feeling what she was feeling. She felt desperate, scared, and hopeless. With a blink of an eye, I was back in my own body. I remember reassuring her, 'I'm going to be ok. I'm going to sort myself out'. I wanted to say anything to release the fear in her eyes, but she was only reflecting the fear she had seen in *my* eyes and her feelings were reflecting my own. I could tell she didn't believe me. But the reassuring words I had spoken to her had planted a seed of determination inside of me: I knew I wanted to do everything I could to be well again.

I didn't have a clue where to start, and I quickly realised there was not going to be a magic wand to fix me. Although my new GP couldn't give me the answers, he supported me to look at my diet and recommended I explore various complementary therapies. I also read every self-help book I could get my hands on. All these things played an instrumental role within my healing journey. But it was a book on Buddhism which became life changing for me – although at first, I almost dismissed it.

The opening chapter of the book began with 'Life is suffering'. I almost didn't make it past these three words and was even tempted to throw the book out the window! Hadn't I already learnt enough about suffering? I kept reading, however, and eventually came upon a chapter about meditation. There it explained how everything in the Universe has its own vibration and by repeating a mantra (i.e., a word or a set of words), we can become the vibration of the mantra. The book suggested I repeat the word *Om*, which is believed to be the sound of the Universe. I felt a huge amount of resistance to repeating *Om*, as I just couldn't relate to it. The media had also portrayed an image of people who meditated as looking cool and calm whilst sitting cross-legged, in kaftans and beads chanting *Om*, and it just wasn't me. I couldn't see myself 'Om-ing'!

I decided it wasn't for me, but as life continued, I couldn't get the thought of meditation and the idea of becoming a different vibration out of my head. I began to wonder what I would like to be, and the words which immediately came to mind were 'happy, healthy and strong'. So, I followed the instructions in the book and picked one of these words at a time as a focus for meditation. Sometimes I found it easy to focus on the word and sometimes it was hard. But I was really hooked. In fact, I began repeating one of the words whenever I could: I would repeat the mantra during sitting meditations, and I would repeat the words whilst brushing my teeth or washing the dishes. Over time, I just started to feel different about myself and my life and I knew it was down to the meditation practice.

But my inner light was still switched off.

'If they are wearing rainbow robes, smelling of patchouli oil and swinging crystals I am going to pretend to get something from my car and drive home,' I said to my boyfriend as I was leaving the house. It was 2003 and I was on my way to meet a reiki master to be attuned to reiki. It had seemed like a great idea when I arranged it, but now doubts were creeping in. Luckily for me, it was a wonderful and supportive environment for taking my first step with reiki. After receiving the reiki attunements (a process of creating a harmonious energetic connection), I felt a deeper understanding of the vibration of my own personal energy. I could see the impact negative thoughts and emotions were having on my mind and body, and how I could work with reiki to release blocked energy. As I walked away from a wonderful two-day experience, I could feel my light beginning to switch back on.

I would use the various techniques I had learnt through meditation and reiki daily to worry less, and I began to focus on what was right in my life instead of focusing on what was wrong. As I became less harsh with myself, I started to treat myself with compassion. I began to practice meditation and reiki daily, and by the end of 2003, I finally let go of the shackles of ME and truly became 'happy, healthy and strong'. The seeds of determination which had been planted during the conversation with my mum had taken root, and I was now beginning to blossom and grow

*

Once I was enjoying the optimum of health and well-being, I felt drawn to support others who were going through a tough time in their life – so after extensive training, I set up a holistic business. This has now developed into a full-time training business helping to empower individuals with their personal and professional development, and in particular, with all aspects of meditation and reiki.

I am also a qualified Kundalini yoga teacher and I start every day with a one-hour practice which I call my 'daily devotion'. This combines yoga and reiki with meditation using breath work, mantra, and chanting. I also ensure I bring loving-kindness, gratitude, and mindfulness into regular moments throughout the day.

My boyfriend, who had supported me throughout ME, is now my husband and we have two amazing boys and a rescue dog. I still play in a band and can occasionally be found stomping around on stage at music festivals. My life is still full of everyday ups and downs and twists and turns, but I can navigate all the changes by utilising everything I have learnt along the way. I know how important it is to look after myself so I can help support those around me. I have also learnt to live in the moment rather than worry about the future or get sad about the past. I am comfortable with my own emotions as well as the emotions of those around me. I understand my introverted ways and I no longer live each day consumed with fear. I treat myself with compassion and I have worked on breaking the temptation to people please. I live my life with a set of principles, based on what I have learned on my journey so far.

In 1999 I was looking at a lifetime of chronic illness consumed with extreme fatigue, anxiety, and depression. But I now live a life where I treat myself as if I am my own best friend, allowing me to access an inner state of calm.

Chapter Two:

Why You Should Meditate

The overwhelm of life

There are times in life when you feel like you are sitting high on a perch knowing exactly where life is leading you. You are in the flow of life, and everything feels as if it is coming together. But then, an unpredictable event will come along and shake the perch and before you know it, you are thrown to the ground below. Sometimes it will feel easy to climb straight back on the perch and carry on as before. Other times you want to lie on the ground and wait to recover before climbing back on. There are even times when you want to stay at the bottom of the perch having a self-pity party. But when the perch has been shaken time and time again, you may feel too fearful to get back on in case you get shaken off once more.

When there are constant knocks it's hard to trust the process of life to unfold in its natural way. Your worries can feel bigger than you and create a blockage in your mind to positive solutions. Fear starts to seep into everyday situations, and tasks which were once easy become an overwhelming effort. Not feeling in control of your life feels like a shameful secret, and you fear others will judge you for not being able to cope. Over-analysing every aspect of your life brings high-level drama to the never-ending stories which play out in your mind.

In some situations, your brain is unable to discern between fact or fiction so will respond accordingly, often drawing you into a fight-or-flight response. This is a primal reaction to protect yourself from perceived dangers. Your heart will race, your breath will become tight and shallow, and the muscles of your body will tense. This heightened state is regulated by the sympathetic nervous system and hormones such as cortisol, adrenaline and noradrenaline will have flooded into the blood stream to produce physiological changes. In other words, your body is providing enough strength and energy, as well as heightened reactions, to help you deal with the danger.

Nowadays we are not presented with as many physical dangers as our prehistoric ancestors. For them, a fight-or-flight reaction would have been a very necessary response. Instead, we are presented constantly with psychological threats, to which our body will respond in the same way.

Most of the psychological threats come from everyday situations, such as the financial pressures of paying the bills and the responsibilities of family life. Work politics and deadlines trickle into home life, whilst disagreements with friends or family can consume everyday living. Extra strain is added if you or a family member suffers with health issues, and you may also have to endure the loss of those you love. You are just a thumb scroll away from constant news headlines, divisive opinions, and the false representation of the perfect life.

As the demands of life build up, not being able to perform the simplest of tasks begins to drive you over the edge, such as not being able to get the lid off a jar of jam. Getting stuck in traffic or sleeping through the alarm can end up ruining your week. When you are unable to find your keys, it can be hard not to take life personally. It can feel as if you have too much to do and too little time to do it in, and you do everything to keep all the plates spinning at the same time.

Overwhelm will set in when you feel you have no control over any aspect of your life. Perhaps you find yourself spending all your time pleasing everyone around you. Fearful of social rejection, it's hard to say no, and you may even feel guilty for taking time out for yourself. Happiness always seems out of reach when the inner critic is often found to be whispering, 'You are not enough'. And to stop the inner loneliness, you make your life busier in the hope it will drown out the internal self-judgement dialogue and the corresponding emotional response.

Over time, as your body continuously responds to both big and small pressures, it can begin to have a detrimental effect on your physical and psychological health. Perhaps you are unable to sleep well, or you are suffering with headaches, muscle tension, or regular colds. Or maybe you are worrying constantly or finding it hard to focus. You might dread going to work or feel depleted when you come back home. Tasks which once seemed easy and straightforward now make you feel overwhelmed, tearful, or irritable. If not dealt with, long term chronic stress can increase the risk of life-changing conditions such as heart disease, diabetes, asthma, gastrointestinal problems, depression, Alzheimer's Disease – just to name a few.

There is another way

In the previous chapter we looked at how chronic stress brought me to meditation, but I haven't explained why I continue to meditate. By the time I was thirty-one, I was enjoying great health and well-being and so it would have been easy to decide to stop meditating. But life took me on another rollercoaster ride.

A week following the birth of my first son, I contracted septicaemia. I was extremely ill at a time when life had already been turned on its head with a newborn baby. Holding my son in my arms moments before I was wheeled down to theatre for an emergency operation, my head was swirling with the melodramatic thought that I wouldn't survive. I tearfully kissed him on the head and said goodbye. Following the operation, I awoke in the recovery room with the flexible breathing tube, which is used to supply oxygen during the op, still in my throat. 'I'm alive', I croaked to the recovery nurse as I mentally performed cartwheels around the room. And as I laid there, I promised myself I would do everything I could to maintain my health and well-being now I was a parent.

I am glad I did, as everyday living is not always easy: there are added pressures as a parent. Not only am I responsible for me, but I also have a responsibility to my two sons (and my rescue dog too.) Maintaining my relationship with my husband needs time and effort now we are parents. I have the bank balance to keep in check and the house to keep in order. Along the way, some of the people I love have had health issues thrown at them – and some I have lost, too. Although I love my work, it still brings along its own stresses.

My meditation practice helps me to navigate through this, bringing calm and equanimity to a life which doesn't know how to stop.

Life is always going to have emotional highs and lows and there is nothing we can do to make ourselves immune to this. It is futile to try to control every aspect of life. Through meditation you learn to roll with the unfolding of each moment as well as how to bend and flex through the difficulties. It becomes easier to dissipate the stress around your negative emotions and you learn to let go of worries and frustrations. Instead of dwelling on your inner critic and self-judgemental dialogue, you begin to connect with your inner confidence and strength, which promotes more positive emotions.

In meditation, you will start to tune into where you hold tension, and you will realise you have a choice over whether you want to hold that tension or let it go. Instead of focusing on the past (which leads to feelings of sadness) or focusing on the future (which leads to feelings of anxiety), you can learn to be in the here and now, more connected to yourself and to what is outside of you. It is through this connection that you will be able to recognise and promote the better sides of yourself. Furthermore, you can learn a technique which will counterbalance the stress in your life and promote a much healthier way of living.

What is meditation?

I initially resisted meditation because I had a preconceived idea of the type of people who meditate. I thought I had to completely silence my mind or be a calm person to be able to do it. I was the opposite of calm; my mind was in a constant state of chatter and the only time it switched off was when I was asleep. Yet even then I would still often wake in the night analysing, processing, judging, worrying, and berating. I thought there was no way I could ever be someone who meditated. It wasn't until I actively gave it a go that I realised it was nothing I had perceived it to be.

Meditation: training your attention

Our minds are designed to process everything going on around us, and this inner dialogue forms the backdrop to our daily experiences. In meditation we are not attempting to silence the inner dialogue. We are instead offering the mind something on which to focus which allows us to be in the present moment. This could be your breath, your body, a word, a phrase, an image, a movement, or an object.

When you bring awareness to the focus, inevitably your mind will become distracted by other things such as thoughts, sounds, and even emotions or discomfort. This is completely normal. The moment you have realised this has happened, without judging yourself in any way, you gently bring your attention back to your chosen focus. When you have noticed the distraction, you are no longer thinking and so it is easier to return to the focus – the noticing is the art of meditation. The repetition of this strengthens your attention to be in the present moment.

Mindfulness: recognising you are the observer

Being sidetracked by your thoughts, sounds, emotions and discomfort is going to be commonplace during meditation as there are so many distractions within and around you. Quite often you will want to act on them in some way too. When you are being drawn into the distractions you are the 'participant' and this is how we spend most of our daily lives, feeling pulled and pushed by the whirlwinds of thoughts, emotions, and feelings. Being in this state means you can often be reactive in the moment and feel you do not have any choice over your actions.

In meditation, you allow yourself some space from being the participant and instead you become the observer of what is happening – this is often referred to as 'open monitoring'. In this observational state you give your attention to whatever arises, when it arises – and so you will be more able to notice your thoughts, your body, your emotions, and the things around you in each moment, without judging, analysing, or creating stories. In other words, you are showing up in the moment you are in, regardless of what is happening and viewing things 'as is'. You will be able to see the difference between the fictional stories you create with your mind and the true reality of the moment. It is only when you are able to see these differences that you are able to dispel the stories and the stress they cause, and realise you have more choice in how you react.

Non-judgement: having a compassionate practice

An important component of meditation is the practice of non-judgment. This is where you will have an acceptance of the moment you are in and view yourself through compassionate eyes. When you hold yourself in this way within your meditation practice, you will know how thoughts, emotions and distractions are always going to come and go. You will only become the thoughts you keep, and in the observational space you will be able to see if you want to act or be defined by them. You will realise you don't have to take whatever is happening in the current moment personally and view instead in a softer and more curious way.

The magic of our brain

In this next section, we are going to look at the physiological and psychological changes which occur when you meditate. Understanding how much meditation can benefit you can help you to feel more invested within the experience.

When I discovered meditation in 2002, I was desperate to find a magic wand to fix my problems and hadn't considered the science behind meditation. The effects on my body, my emotions, my mental well-being, and my spirit – on just about everything – felt magical. When I trained to be a meditation teacher, I discovered this magical effect came from the physiological and psychological changes which were happening within my brain and in my body. And all these changes can be proven. With this knowledge, you too can connect more deeply with your practice, and see why this investment in yourself is so important.

Meditation will release the stress from your body

Would you like to be able to counterbalance the stress in your body? In meditation, as you begin to focus on a breath, word or image, your brain will begin to receive signals showing there is no threat or danger around you, and balance out the fight-or-flight response. Your heart rate and blood pressure will lower, and your breathing rate will decrease. Blood will flow more easily to your muscles to release tension, and your digestion will improve. This is due to your parasympathetic nervous system becoming activated and releasing chemicals and brain signals. All the systems of the body can now calm, helping with feelings of anxiety.

Named the 'relaxation response' by Dr Herbert Benson, a medical doctor, cardiologist and founder of the Mind/Body Medical Institute at Massachusetts General Hospital in Boston, USA, it is the perfect antidote to stress and the fight-or-flight response.

Meditation will re-wire your brain, so you respond differently to stress

Would you like to respond differently to stress? Experience changes your brain, so when you are training your attention with focused awareness in meditation, new connections and neurons are created. Prior to the discovery of neuroplasticity, it was believed that once the brain had fully formed it couldn't change. But thanks to advances in scientific research into meditation, we now know that even a small amount of practice can induce measurable changes in the brain that can be tracked on a brain scanner.

We can use the analogy of taking a walk through the woods to understand this: the path you take on your daily walk isn't the most exciting path, but it's the one that has become most trodden. One day, you look through the trees and you see a beautiful spot next to a river. The sun is shining on the water and there are lovely plants and trees. But you can't get there as there are so many trees and brambles in your way. On your next walk, you decide to cut back the trees and the brambles so you can make your way to the beautiful spot. It isn't easy but it is worth it, and when you reach the spot you are glad you did it. The next day, when you return, the brambles have grown back over and you must cut them back again, but you continue to repeat this every day and, little by little, it becomes easier to walk the new path. Eventually, you realise the old trodden path has grown over and the only path you want to walk is the one to the beautiful spot.

It is the same with meditation. With chronic stress your neurons are going to be in a vigilant state, and will take you along the now familiar path of fight-or-flight (path most trodden). However, the more you train your attention through meditation (cut back the brambles), the more you will introduce the relaxation response which slows the systems of the body down and creates a calmer response to stress (taking you to the beautiful spot). Eventually, when faced with stress your brain will recognise that meditation techniques bring calm (the new path). For this to be most effective, meditation needs to become a regular and consistent practice.

Meditation will give you a thicker brain

Would you like to have a younger brain with improved focus and a better memory? Would you like to have better emotional processing with improved empathy and compassion for yourself and others? Would you also like to feel less fearful? A regular, and consistent, meditation practice will give you all of this.

The 'thicker brain' relates to the grey matter in the brain, which normally thins as we get older. Yet studies have noted how fifty-year-old meditators had the same amount of grey matter as twenty-five-year-olds. And the great news about grey matter doesn't stop there: since 2005 neuroscientist Sara Lazar and her team at Harvard University and Massachusetts General Hospital have led pioneering studies in the world of meditation. Initial research showed more grey matter in the auditory and sensory cortex, demonstrating that when you are focusing on your breath, your senses are enhanced. This shows you will be more able to be present with your physical sensations and the sounds around you. But in addition to this, the study also showed more grey matter in the left pre-frontal cortex, an area associated with working memory (meaning we will retain the ability to store temporary information and not lose track of what we are doing) and executive decision making (so we can plan, focus our attention, remember instructions and multi task).

A further study demonstrated a thickening in the left hippocampus (involved in learning, memory and emotional regulation), and the temporoparietal junction (the area involved with empathy and perspective taking).

When we get older, the amygdala – the emotional processing part of the brain which decides if a fight-or-flight response is required – gets bigger. The amygdala is unable to discern between a real threat and a perceived one. This will mean the stressful thoughts we have, or the stories or movies we create in our minds, will be enough to trigger the fight-or-flight, inducing feelings of anxiety, fear, anger, and stress. Interestingly, the studies demonstrated a shrinking of grey matter, which correlated with a reduction in stress levels. So, when we practice meditation regularly, we are less likely to feel fearful.

Brain waves and meditation

Brain waves are rhythmic patterns of neural activity in the central nervous system measured on an electroencephalogram (EEG), and show us the frequency of waves per second, known as hertz (Hz). There are five categories of brain waves.

The fastest rates of brain waves, Gamma waves, measure between 35–100 Hz. When you are intensely focused the brain waves tend to oscillate at a faster rate. Research has shown how these brain waves allow different parts of the brain to communicate and create an overall picture.

Our everyday brainwaves, Beta waves, oscillate at a frequency of between 13–32 Hz. This indicates an active, busy, and sometimes anxious state of mind, which means we are alert and processing what is going on around us.

When we are relaxed, we have slower brain activity called Alpha waves (8–13 Hz). This is the entry state of sleep, where you are aware of sounds and thoughts, but you aren't really processing their meanings.

When we are asleep and dreaming we are in the Theta state (4–8 Hz), and when we are in a dreamless sleep we experience delta (0.5–4 Hz).

Would you like to have calmer brain waves? When you start to meditate, your brain waves begin to slow down and move through to the alpha relaxed state, where you begin to feel unattached to your thoughts and what is going on around you – this is often referred to as relaxed wakefulness. Beyond this there can also be theta wave activity which can often lead to a 'blissful' type feeling – in particular theta waves indicate a deep relaxation.

Interestingly, scientists have been able to see gamma waves in experienced meditators, combined with alpha and theta waves. This indicates a heightened perception and is often felt like a shift in consciousness – in other words an 'a-ha' lightbulb moment.

*

These are just some of the many scientific discoveries which demonstrate the physiological changes to the body and brain, and there are many other studies which look at how meditation can benefit mental and physical health and well-being. Hopefully, with this knowledge, you will now be able to take a more invested look at how meditation can play a part in supporting you.

It is a wonder why meditation isn't practised in every household in the country. Certainly, a lot of health professionals are seeing the benefits and recommending a regular practice to their patients as a way of encouraging personal responsibility for health and well-being. Yet in some cases, there can be resistance to this – which we will look at in the next chapter.

Chapter Three:

What is Getting in Your Way?

Overcoming the resistance

In chapter one I mentioned how I didn't want to 'Om' and sit in a kaftan, so I had already decided meditation wasn't for me. But this isn't the whole picture. By the time I was reading the book on Buddhism, I had accepted I wasn't going to find quick fix to recovering from ME. The path to wellness was already proving to be long, and I had taken some wrong turns along the way. I read the chapter about mantras, and I began to feel quite hopeful. But as I continued to read the book, I opened myself to a tiny whisper of fear which told me I might not be good at meditating and it might not work for me. This fear then released a tsunami of resistance to the thought of trying something new.

You may wish to learn to mediate and have already recognised how it can help your life, but you may have the same fears as me. Or you may be worried it will take up too much of your time, energy, and motivation; perhaps you are planning to read this book through and then do the meditation practice when you create some spare time in your life – on your next holiday, or when work calms down a bit. Or you are hoping life will become a bit calmer before you can 'life' better, but underneath you may already feel guilty about spending time on yourself. You might have decided you are not the right 'type' of person to meditate as you are not very calm and won't be able to silence your mind. Perhaps you are concerned you don't have the right equipment or space to do it in. Or you may be frightened of change.

In this chapter we are going to address obstacles which may be getting in the way of doing something new.

'I feel guilty if I spend any time on myself'

You will not have been born into this feeling of guilt about spending time on yourself, but along the way it may have been ingrained into your psyche. Perhaps you now consider the idea selfish or self-indulgent, or that spare time should be spent with family or catching up on work deadlines, or even DIY projects. Maybe your inner critic casts shameful judgments on you for even *thinking* about having any time to yourself, telling you it is a clear sign that you don't appreciate your family, job, or home.

To put a 'selfish' label on yourself would imply you are doing something for yourself at the expense of others – but this couldn't be further from the truth. Putting the needs of everyone else before yourself can result in you becoming drained and unhappy. Surely this way of living comes at your expense?

Meditation is an investment in yourself. If the techniques help you to feel calm, relaxed, and less stressed, this will benefit everyone around you. By meditating, you are creating a win-win situation for you and the people you care about.

'I'm not sure I have time to fit this in'

There are not enough hours in the day to get things done as it is, and now you are going to be adding something extra. Just the thought can bring a wave of anxiety. But what if you were more effective with your time? Many people who meditate report that they are able to manage their time much more effectively – and scientific research shows that it may lead to better focus and levels of concentration.

When we are children, we often can't see the importance of cleaning our teeth – but as adults we commit to it at least a couple of times a day as we see it as a practical investment in gum health. Is there any reason why you couldn't think the same about your mental and physical health? Rather than adding it onto the never-ending list of jobs, why not schedule it in and make it a priority? It doesn't need to take up lots of time – you can always start small and begin to build up. Plus, when you meditate you may find you are able to tackle all your other tasks more easily.

There isn't a perfect time to meditate; it really is going to be down to you to create a small amount of time to do it. Some people find it best to meditate in the morning and some even set their alarm a little earlier. Some meditate in the evening before going to bed, some at lunchtime. If you do it at the same time every day, it makes it easier to commit to it regularly.

'I can't silence my mind'

If you are consumed with overwhelming thoughts on a daily basis and you haven't found the 'off' switch, how are you going be able to stop the incessant chatter when you meditate?

Our brains are designed to process the stimuli around us so trying to force your mind into silence can cause quite a bit of stress. It is believed we have between 40,000 to 80,000 thoughts and feelings per day, some of which are positive, some negative, but most are quite mundane and form the chitter-chattering backdrop of your processing mind. These thoughts are not interesting enough to form an attachment to.

Meditation is not about silencing the mind. Instead, you will be offering your mind a concentrated focus, such as your breath or a word. At some point, maybe after only a few seconds, your mind will naturally become distracted by a thought, feeling, sound or an ache or pain in the body. Once you realise you have become distracted, without judging yourself, you gently come back to the concentrated focus.

With the practice of returning to the concentrated focus, you begin to notice there are pauses which occur between thoughts. Normally we are too busy to notice they exist. But with meditation you will have the space to witness this pause and view it as a natural silence which exists within you.

'I'm not a calm person'

Perhaps you feel you are a fiery and reactive person –the opposite to the uber calm and peaceful person who is sat cross-legged in a beautiful setting next to a still lake. These are the images depicted by the media who are attempting to sell you a lifestyle. In reality, most people who seek out meditation are looking to curb their strong reactions.

As you discovered in the previous chapter, the mindfulness part of the practice allows you space between what is happening and your reaction, enabling you to see that you have choice over what you hold on to and what you let go. On top of the physiological changes which meditation can bring, you will begin to feel much more able to connect with the calm and peaceful feelings which also reside within you.

'I can't sit in a lotus position'

Sitting in lotus position involves placing both feet on opposite thighs. Through many years of yoga training this can be achieved (or if you have flexible hips) – but is not a necessity for the practice itself. The idea behind this position is to set a grounded mountain posture for the practice: your buttocks and the balancing of your knees on the floor offer a tripod effect so the body can sit in a natural way above it – just like the mountain sits above its base. You can achieve the same grounded effect by sitting on a cushion, stool, or even a chair. Not all meditations are in sitting posture; some can be done lying down or through movement.

To start with, a chair will most likely feel comfortable, plus your practice will feel much more portable (if you associate meditation with lying down, you might always feel you will have to lie down to be able to do it). With a sitting practice you will be able to meditate on a train, plane, in the car (not while driving!) – anywhere and everywhere.

Here are some tips to get you started in a sitting chair posture:

To create a sense of being grounded, place both feet on the floor. If your feet do not reach the floor, place them on a cushion. Bring awareness to the contact points of your feet and the surface they are on.

1. Sit up straight, but not in a rigid way – think of pebbles that have been stacked on top of one another on a beach. That is how you want to picture your back, with the natural curvature at the bottom of your spine. You can always place

a cushion behind your back should you need the extra support.

2. Let your hands rest naturally on your thighs, palms facing up or down. Or if you prefer, you can cup one hand over the other or clasp them together. Allow your chin to be tilted slightly down.
3. Relax your shoulders and allow them to slip down and away from your ears. Relax your jaw (if your jaw is tense, it is likely all the other joints in your body will be tense too). You can always give your jaw a little wriggle to loosen any tension.
4. Rest your eyes on a fixed spot on the floor or wall, or you can close your eyes. If you choose to have your eyes open, allow your gaze to be soft and relaxed.

'What if I am not any good at it, I do it wrong, or it doesn't work for me?'

We often have a fear of failure when starting something new. We can also fear success. Society has given us this measure, so we often label things as 'good' or 'bad', 'right' or 'wrong'. But this goal-oriented approach of being a success or being good at something doesn't work within a mediation practice. In fact, these labels will act like a stop sign in the moment-to-moment flow of the practice.

The truth of the practice is sometimes you will find it easy to maintain focus: you may feel 'in the zone' and even when your mind is distracted it will feel easy to bring it back to the focus again. But sometimes the practice will be hard, with an ever-increasing circle of thoughts swirling around in an interlocking chain. This may create feelings of annoyance and irritation with yourself, leading to a tensing of your body. You might even feel as if the volume has been turned up on every sound – ones you hadn't ever noticed before. And then your clothes start to feel heavy on your skin and you can feel the fabric of your socks between your toes!

It doesn't mean it is not working – nor that you are doing it wrong, it is just how this moment in the practice is unfolding. Quite often, when it is hard, you are actually learning lots about the practice itself and your own reactions. And remember, when you are able to see this, you will begin to realise you have space and choice in how you wish to respond.

Meditation is training your attention, so the key is how you treat yourself within the practice. If your mind wanders a thousand times, the moment you notice you gently bring it back a thousand times. That is the true essence of meditating.

'I'm frightened it will change me'

Change can feel scary for most of us. Rather than changing you, it is a set of tools to help you notice what is happening so you can navigate your life better. You will not be adopting a new personality overnight, as it is an evolving practice and you evolve with it – after more than twenty years of meditating, I still do not own a kaftan! There is no pressure to change; you will simply notice what is taking place moment to moment instead.

To use the phrase by author Susan Jeffers, sometimes you just have to 'feel the fear and do it anyway'.

Now we have addressed the obstacles, you will be able to view your own resistance with truth and honesty and in this present moment you know you have choice: to stay with the resistance or to let it go and take the next step into your meditation experience – and into the first of the meditations in the next chapter.

Chapter Four:

Foundation: Breath

The breath is your friend

Every moment of every day you are breathing – but when do you notice it? Perhaps you are aware of it now as I have just mentioned it, but are there other times when you notice the air coming in and out of your body? You may only notice your breath when your lungs are complaining, such as when you are walking, cycling, attempting to run up a hill, or when a cold has turned into a chest infection. There may also be times when you are nervous, anxious, or fearful and it brings a tightness or breathlessness to your lungs.

When I had ME, my lungs often felt narrow and constricted and it would feel as if I was breathing through a straw. In meetings where I had once spoken confidently, and in between songs during gigs, the shortness of breath would get in the way of my words, driving my anxiety into full-blown panic attacks.

It's natural to feel alarmed when we can't get a full feeling of breath. In fact, it's in these times we feel as if breath is working against us – an enemy of sorts. But what happens if you concentrate on your breath at other times?

Within the first ten seconds of being born you take your first breath, and then every breath after this becomes an involuntary function where your brain controls the flow of air. Without having to think about it, the breath is always there for you, so this makes a good starting point for a meditation practice. As Sharon Salzberg, co-founder of Insight Meditation Society, says, 'if you can breathe, you can meditate.'

But first, let's remind ourselves of how the breath brings physiological calm to the body instead of fear. In chapter two, we learnt how the simple art of focusing on the breath activates the relaxation response, which is the perfect counterbalance to stress. So instead of viewing the breath as the enemy, you can begin to view it as a friend.

Within a breath meditation you will experience how your body breathes naturally. Therefore, the breath is used as a focused attention point: you direct your awareness of it coming into the body and then back out again. You choose where, on your body, to settle your focus. Your attention may be on your mouth, your upper lip or on the tip of your nose as you feel the air drifting past. You might focus on the movement of air travelling up through the nostrils and then back out again. You may follow the journey of the breath as it moves through the nostrils, through the throat, and into the lungs, before exhaling the air back out again. Or all of your focus could be on the sensation of your lungs inflating and then deflating.

Alternatively, your focused attention can be on the movement of your muscles as you breathe. This could be noticing how the muscles in your chest wall move up and down, or being aware of the muscles in your abdomen rising as you breathe in and falling back towards your spine as you breathe out.

You will notice how the rhythm of your breath is always changing, and there are often little pauses which occur very naturally. You may also be aware of tingling or pressure. Sometimes the breath is smooth, sometimes it is ragged. But the aim is to witness the breath during each moment.

Why not give it a go now?

Take a few breaths, with complete awareness. You don't need to change your breath, just simply notice the breath coming in and then going out of your body.

Awareness of breath coming in . . .

Awareness of breath going out . . .

Awareness of breath coming in . . .

Awareness of breath going out . . .

Awareness of breath coming in . . .

Awareness of breath going out . . .

Well done – you did it! During these six simple breaths, you might have found your mind wandered a little, which is normal.

Some people feel a bit unnerved noticing the breath, and this is understandable. If the breath has felt like the enemy for so long, it will feel strange to focus on it now. You can always remind yourself the breath will be inviting calm to your body and set an intention to be gentle with yourself. And, instead of focusing on the sensation of the breath, you can mentally note, 'I am breathing in, I am breathing out' instead. This way, the focus is on the words rather than the sensation.

Now let's do it for a little longer . . .

Let's meditate: awareness of breath

Listen to this audio meditation at sarahpresley.co.uk/making-friends-with-yourself/meditations

Sitting comfortably, allow your eyes to gently close or place your gaze on a fixed spot in the room: this can be a wall or the floor. Go with what feels right for you.

Allow your body to be held by the surface you are resting on, so you can rest in your experience.

Begin to pay attention to the breath coming in and out of your body – don't change it in any way, just notice yourself breathing naturally . . . simply noticing your breath coming into your body, and then going back out . . . .

Perhaps you notice your breath at your mouth, your upper lip, or at the tip of your nose. You may feel the sensation of your breath as it comes up through your nostrils and back out again. You might even notice the temperature, either a coolness or warmth as you breathe. . . .

Maybe you follow your breath up through your nostrils, through your throat to your lungs before you exhale and release . . . .

Or you might be aware of the movement of the muscles in your chest wall, or how your lungs expand and deflate. Or aware of how your belly rises as you breathe in and falls back towards your spine as you breathe out . . . .

You might feel pressure or movement or something else. Just let yourself breath naturally, without forcing or changing it in any way. You are always breathing, and in this moment, you are noticing . . . .

If it helps to steady your attention, you can always label the breath. 'I am breathing in, I am breathing out' or simply 'in, out . . . .'

If your mind wanders, it's OK. When you are ready, gently bring it back to the focus of the breath. The art of meditation is in the noticing of being distracted. Wherever you go – whether it is to your thoughts, feelings or sounds around you – you can very gently return to your breath . . . .

You can trust your body to breathe for you and you may even notice how your breath is bringing calmness to your body . . . .

But sometimes there can be things around us which draw our attention away, such as thoughts, emotions, sounds or discomfort. It's OK. The moment you realise you are not with your breath gently bring it back again. There is no need to judge. You are training your attention to be in the current moment . . . .

Sometimes it is easy to focus on the breath, sometimes it is hard. But there is no right or wrong to this experience. Just be gentle with yourself and the moment you realise you are distracted, come back one breath at a time . . . .

Simply breathing in and breathing out . . . .

Now, when you feel ready, be aware of your body and the surface it is resting on and aware of your breath at your nose. Then, in your own time, you can gently open your eyes.

You have done it – you have meditated! You may have found it easy to follow the breath, or you may have found it hard – we can naturally be distracted by wandering thoughts meaning you had to repeatedly return to the breath, but either way is perfect as you are training your attention. Obviously, it can feel great when your focus feels really switched on, but the point is the noticing and bringing it back – this means you are meditating.

Did you judge yourself for thinking?

It is natural to think when you are meditating. In fact, it will probably happen seconds into the practice. However, if you judge yourself for thinking, it will stop the meditation flow as it may raise a strong emotion such as irritation or frustration. Or you might feel worried you are not doing it right or are unable to do it at all.

We are used to judging the experiences in our lives as good or bad, right, or wrong, or even as success or failure. In meditation there is no such thing as a bad, wrong or a failing meditation practice. The emphasis is on the word 'practice' – you are practicing being in the present moment. Sometimes it will feel easy to be in the present moment and sometimes it will be hard. But even when it is hard, you are still learning about yourself – as well as the practice.

Shunryu Suzuki, a Zen monk and teacher, says, 'Leave your front door and your back door open. Allow your thoughts to come and go. Just don't serve them tea'. So, if you are finding yourself thinking (drinking tea), notice and let go of the thought (pop the teacup down), and return to your breath (open the front and back door).

Distracting thoughts and feelings are always going to be there, but the practice will allow you to let them go and return to noticing the breath coming in, and then going back out again. Simply put, as you breathe, notice you've been distracted, and then return to the breath. After a while you will find the breath will be the anchor to each unfolding moment.

Each time you practice a breath meditation it will feel different. If you found it hard the first time, you could always do it again another time as the next experience may be different. If you feel this meditation is not for you, don't worry, it doesn't mean you are not able to meditate. It just means it isn't the right fit for you right now. I often think of the different types of meditations like shoes – we must try them on to see if we like them. Try this pair of shoes on a few times and if you find it is not for you, there are plenty of other pairs to try on (and we will be discovering them in later chapters.) If you did enjoy the breath meditation, there are still some others you can explore.

Using the breath to bring down scattered thoughts and energy

Anxiousness causes the breath to become short and shallow and is accompanied by scattered energy and thinking. With a diaphragmatic breathing meditation, you can actively make the breath slower and longer, so your body and mind are able to feel relaxed and calmer. You do this by focusing on the movement of the diaphragm.

The diaphragm is a muscle situated just below your lungs and heart and is the primary muscle used in respiration. When you breathe in, the muscle contracts and moves downwards creating more space for the lungs to fill with air. Then when you breathe out the muscle relaxes and goes back up, helping the lungs to release air.

As well as bringing the relaxation response to the body, this technique will help to strengthen the diaphragm and stabilise core muscles.

Let's practice this now.

Let's meditate: belly breathing meditation

Listen to this audio meditation at sarahpresley.co.uk/making-friends-with-yourself/meditations

Sitting comfortably, allow your eyes to gently close or place your gaze on a fixed spot in the room: this can be a wall or the floor. Go with what feels right for you.

Allow your body to be held by the surface you are resting on, so you can rest in your experience.

Begin to pay attention to the breath coming in and out of your body – don't change it in anyway, just notice yourself breathing in your natural way . . . .

If it helps, you can always silently say 'aware of my breath coming in, aware of my breath going out' to steady your attention . . . .

We are going to take a purposeful journey down the body until we reach the diaphragm. So, start now by noticing the breath at your nose. Maybe you are aware of the breath at the tip, or the journey it takes up and down your nostrils. You might be aware of the temperature or the movement . . . .

Take a few breaths here, just noticing. And if your mind wanders, just allow the breath to steady your attention . . . .

Now, bring your awareness to the journey of your breath as it moves up through your nostrils

into your throat and then into your lungs, before exhaling and releasing. Maybe here you notice your lungs inflating and deflating. Or the movement of the muscles on your chest wall as you breathe. Maybe you feel an openness or pressure . . . .

Take a few breaths, just noticing. And if you are feeling distracted, gently let go of the distractions and come back to your breath . . . .

Now, bring your awareness to your belly, perhaps noticing here how your abdomen rises as you breathe in and goes back towards your spine as you breathe out. Maybe you feel a rhythmic movement here, or maybe the breaths feel uneven. Just continue to follow the rising as you breathe in, and the falling as you breathe out . . . .

As you continue to focus your attention here you may feel a fuller breath, or maybe the breath feels deeper and slower . . . .

If it helps to steady your attention, you could silently say 'belly' on your in breath and 'relax' on your out breath.

Belly . . . Relax . . .

Belly . . . Relax . . .

Belly . . . Relax . . .

Keeping your attention on your abdomen with each breath, continue this practice . . . .

.

.

•

If your mind wanders, just gently come back to, belly . . . relax . . .

•

•

•

Now be aware of your body and the surface it is resting on and aware of your breath at your nose. Then, in your own time, you can gently open your eyes.

I was once invited to give a talk about meditation to school teachers during their staff meeting. It was an unfamiliar environment and I felt outside of my comfort zone, which induced a spiky ball of anxiousness in the pit of my stomach. Bringing awareness to this, I practiced the diaphragmatic breathing technique until I could feel the spiky ball beginning to soften and I felt much calmer. I did all of this with my eyes open, so no one in the room knew I was practicing meditation.

Bringing meditation to the everyday

As we have seen in this chapter, the breath is an excellent way to focus your attention and bring calmness to your body, but you do not always need to wait until you are in a sitting posture to practice breathing awareness. In fact, you could bring conscious breathing exercises into a variety of moments throughout the day.

When teaching meditation, I often mention this, and some of the best ideas for conscious breathing exercises have come from my students. Here are a couple:

The door handle

Lisa had a high-powered job, involving back-to-back meetings. She had often felt there was no let up and the demands on her time felt relentless. When experiencing the breath meditation for the first time, she felt instant relief and wanted to find a way to bring this into her busy day. Her idea was to use the door handle on each office door as a reminder to connect with the calm she had experienced in the meditation: she decided she would place her hand onto the door handle and take three conscious breaths before stepping into her next meeting. A few weeks later, she was amazed at the difference this was bringing to her day – so much so that she introduced the concept to her colleagues.

Chapters in the day

Being a mum to four children, Gemma often found herself saying 'I don't have time to breathe'. Learning the short conscious breath exercise meant she could bring the practice into bite-sized chunks in her day. She began viewing each stage of the day like chapters of a book: the morning chapter was getting everyone up, fed and dressed;

the next chapter was taking the older children to school; another was taking her middle child to preschool; and the next chapter was bringing her youngest child back home, continuing with many more chapters throughout the day. Now she could take three conscious breaths at the start of each new chapter and enter the next part of the day feeling less overwhelmed.

You may want to consider adding an alarm to your phone so it chimes a reminder to do some conscious breathing on every hour of the day, or you could use the checking of your social media pages or emails as a prompt for your breaths. There are many natural opportunities throughout the day where you can make the connection with yourself, such as taking the opportunity to breathe at a red traffic light when in the car, standing in line at the supermarket, or waiting for a document to be printed in the office. All you need to do is have awareness of the breath coming in and out of the body, in its natural way, for only a few breaths.

In this chapter, you have taken the first step to be in each unfolding moment. The more you practice, the more you will be witnessing what is happening in the here and now, without buying into the distractions of thoughts and feelings about the past or future. You now have the first foundation which can be used within other meditations, as you take the journey to a calmer mind and body.

Chapter Five:

Making Friends With Anxiety

Outside of work one day, I was sat in my car dreading the thought of walking into the office, and I felt the full force of fear gripping me. My breathing became rapid and shallow, and I thought my heart was going to pump out of my chest. Pinned to my seat, my stomach tensed and my toes rolled up in my shoes. The car felt like it was closing in on me and I felt trapped – I wanted to flee but I was unable to move.

I was having a full-blown anxiety attack.

This was not unusual, as I often had anxiety attacks in my car outside of the office. Sometimes I would find a release to the anxiety by bursting into tears, other times I would drive home on autopilot. I didn't realise at the time how work had become like a lion's den: I feared not being able to complete work deadlines and being shouted at by my boss; I feared the judgement of my colleagues and how they would realise I was an imposter and didn't know how to do my job; I was also fearful about how much my health was deteriorating in my quest to always do my best, working long hours to achieve the unachievable. I was on a hamster wheel and I didn't know how to get off it.

Anxiety was an unwelcome life passenger which had arrived because my body and mind had become over stressed. Everyday tasks which had once seemed so simple started to seem dangerous, even life threatening, and I was in a constant state of alert. Eventually, the surge of overwhelm and fear lead to the unpleasant experience of anxiety attacks, which began to come with regularity and without warning.

On this particular occasion, however, something changed. I had already been meditating at home for a few months at this point, and a tiny thought dropped into my consciousness, saying, 'this will soon pass'. I immediately knew I didn't need to buy into the stress of the situation, and so I encouraged myself to take a few conscious deep breaths – allowing the *out* breath to be slightly longer than the *in* breath, my body started to respond. I could feel a slither of calmness begin to wash over me, along with a glimmer of hope that I might finally be able to take back some control.

Understanding your relationship with anxiety

When you are in an anxious spiral it doesn't seem possible to step out. But when I reflected afterwards, I realised that the panic I had felt was a small moment in time compared to the rest of the day. Yet every time it happened, I had always allowed it to affect me mentally and physically for a long time after: my mind would be like a stuck record replaying the anxiety, and my body would be tensed and braced in case it happened again.

I also realised by repeating the word 'anxiety' to myself made me feel anxious so, to help me understand my relationship with it, I gave it a new name. From now on, I would refer to anxiety as 'Mavis'!

The moment I changed the name, the intensity of the anxious feeling shifted like a movement of energy. It felt transformational and although it was a small step, I knew I was beginning to break the cycle. If you were to start this chapter again and change all the 'anxiety' words to 'Mavis' you would know exactly what I mean.

Giving anxiety a new name now meant I could view the part of myself which was feeling anxious and scared. I would be more aware of when Mavis was arriving and be able to engage the rational part of my brain to ask if the situation I was in required a visit from her. Or even if she had already stormed in, I was able to ride out her visit knowing she would be leaving soon after. After all, she was just doing her best job to protect me from what she perceived as danger.

I realised the overwhelming feeling of panic wasn't attempting to trip me up but instead was giving me something I could use to learn and grow. Most importantly, I accepted and made peace with Mavis being in my life.

I had gained this perspective due to the space meditation was giving me. Through training my attention, I was more able to allow each moment to unfold, helping me to realise how all moments are impermanent – meaning they are temporary. With meditation I was the observer, and I was able to view anxiety and how it plays out in my mind and body. I was also able to reflect more easily on situations without buying into any negative and destructive thoughts.

You might not want to name your anxiety, but in this chapter we are going to look at why you feel it and look at another meditation which can help your concentrated focus.

What is anxiety?

Anxiety arrives when you are feeling apprehensive, uneasy, or fearful about what is about to happen. It is a natural way to feel and is a very human response to perceiving yourself to be in a vulnerable situation. You normally feel it when you are in situations outside of your comfort zone –and a little of anxiety can actually be a good thing, helping you stay alert and focused.

Although it is a natural reaction, it is a persistent feeling of anxiety which can lead to both physiological and psychological problems. You may find you can't shake the feeling and it begins to impact your sleep. You might need your loved ones to provide constant reassurance with any decisions you make. Or you may feel hyper alert and unable to relax.

From a physiological point of view, you may experience a pounding or palpitating heart. Your stomach may feel like it is constantly churning, and you need to go to the toilet more often. Your breath may feel like it has sped up and you feel you are sweating more.

Anxiety is a result of the over activation of the fight-or-flight response – if you are unable to find the means to calm down (i.e. decreasing the grey matter density in the amygdala, the emotional processing part of the brain) then you can feel like you're in a constant stressed state. Meditation is the way in which you can calm this down.

Scientific research into meditation has proven it can help with anxiety. Neuroscientists discovered that when meditating, the brain waves in the stress-prone right frontal cortex move to the calmer left cortex. This is good news for mild depression, too. There is also evidence to show there is less activity in the amygdala, the area of the brain which processes fear.

Introducing mantra meditation

One of the meditations I found to be helpful for my anxiety was the mantra meditation. This was the first meditation I discovered after reading a book on Buddhism. The word 'mantra' comes from two Sanskrit words: *man*, which means mind, and *tra*, which means vehicle or instrument. In this meditation you repeat a phrase or word and, rather than focus on the meaning, you focus on the repetition. In other words, the repetition of the word is a 'mind vehicle' you use to replace your thoughts.

Everything is in a constant state of vibration – including ourselves as well as inanimate objects. This vibration has resonance, some which is audible and some which is not. Sound in particular can be evocative and can have an impact on how we feel. Through the repetition of the mantra, the vibration can be transformational and have an impact on your thoughts and emotions and also go deeper into your consciousness. You can effectively become at one with the vibration of the mantra.

Mantras can be words which have meaning, or they can be meaningless. The emphasis is on the vibration and sound, and they can be chanted, whispered, or repeated silently in the mind.

The act of repeating the mantra is known as *japa*, which translates as 'muttering, whispering', where the mantra becomes the focus of your attention. Just like you were focusing on the breath in chapter five, you now focus on your chosen word. And just like the breath meditation induces the relaxation response to your body and mind, so too will the mantra.

Choosing a mantra

Even though it has links to Hinduism and Buddhism, you do not need to have any spiritual beliefs to enjoy this type of meditation. It is a practice open to all.

When picking a mantra, the best option is to choose something you can connect with. Research has shown it doesn't matter what you repeat, you will still get the same results, so a familiar word can be a good start. In mantra meditation we call these 'meaningful words', and you could choose, for example: calm, peace, strong, love, confident, serene, content, relax.

What word has true meaning for you right now? When I asked this question to myself before I started to meditate, I had three words which came to mind: I wanted to feel happy, healthy and strong. I would focus on one of these each time I meditated.

If you would like a more spiritual connection, you can use a word from your own faith. Alternatively, there are also Vedic meaningful mantras such as *so 'ham* meaning I am that, or *sat-cit-anada*, meaning truth, consciousness, bliss. *Om (Aum)* is another well-known mantra which is considered to be the constant sound of the Universe.

Alternatively, you could pick a meaningless mantra such as a soothing sound like 'ahhhh' or 'mmmm'. Many sound practitioners believe these sounds will relax the muscles around your jaw, neck and chest, washing away tension. In addition to this, they also suggest humming will send calming messages to your nervous system due to the larynx (vocal box) being connected to your vagus nerve.

When you first start repeating the mantra, your mind and body might give you many reasons not to repeat your word or phrase. For instance, if you pick calm, you may find your mind isn't calm nor is your body. But isn't that the reason you picked calm in the first place? Didn't you pick it because it was the opposite of how you currently feel? So, if your mind and body give you reason not to feel calm, let these reasons go and return to calm. When repeating the mantra, there is no need to think about the meaning of the word. Instead, focus on the repetition of your chosen word so it becomes a meaningless sound. When you focus on the vibrational quality you will find it much easier to disconnect from what is going on around you.

Let's meditate: mantra meditation – calm

Listen to this audio meditation at sarahpresley.co.uk/making-friends-with-yourself/meditations

Sitting comfortably, allow your eyes to gently close or place your gaze on a fixed spot in the room: this can be a wall or the floor.

Allow your body to be held by the surface you are resting on, so you can rest in your experience.

In your own time, and in your own way, take a long deep breath in . . . . and then release it when you are ready . . . . Now allow your attention to focus on your natural breath . . . .

Bring to mind the word 'calm' and begin to repeat it inside your mind . . . . Allow the best

rhythm for you – it can be on the breath, on the in-breath, the out-breath, or even both. Or you can repeat at your own rhythm: it can be fast or slow, or somewhere in between.

Allow the word 'calm' to be the focus of your attention.

Your mind might give you many reasons not to repeat the word calm, but let those reasons go and come back to calm. Connect with the repetition of the word rather than the meaning . . . .

We are going to take a journey around the body with the mantra. Everywhere we place our attention, we are going to repeat the word calm. So, bring your awareness to the crown of your head as you continue to repeat calm . . . . now bring it to the back of your head . . . your face . . . then your throat and neck . . .

Now bring it to your shoulders . . . the tops of your arms . . .. your forearms . . . your hands, fingers, and thumbs . . .

Bring calm to the top of your back . . . the middle . . . and then the bottom of your back . . .

Now bring it to your chest . . . and then your abdomen . . . .Next, bring it to your pelvis . . . your thighs . . . your knees . . . your lower legs . . . feet and toes . . .

Now bring it to the space behind your forehead, and let it rest there, as you continue to repeat calm . . . .

Sometimes it will feel easy to focus on calm, sometimes it will feel hard. But don't worry, wherever you go, whatever happens just bring yourself back to calm . . . .

.

.

.

It is time to release the mantra, so come back to focusing on your breath for a few more moments . . . .

Be aware of the surface your body is being supported by. And when you feel ready, gently open your eyes.

Well done – you've done it! And remember, sometimes it will feel easy, sometimes it will feel hard. It's just the nature of the practice right now. But wherever you are is a starting point.

In this meditation we brought the vibration of the word around the body, but you don't have to do this each time. You can just repeat the mantra silently in your mind and simply bring your focus back whenever it wanders, should you prefer.

You also don't have to be sat in meditation; you could repeat your mantra to yourself anytime. It could be whilst doing the dishes or cleaning your teeth. Even if for a short while, it will still have a positive effect on your mind and body.

Hopefully, by understanding your relationship with anxiety, you can now begin to take further steps to making friends with yourself. In the next chapter we are going to put down the next foundation for our meditation practice and look at how we can connect with our bodies in a more positive way.

Chapter Six:

Foundation: Body

Your body is your friend

When I was nineteen, I was diagnosed with dyspraxia, a disorder which affects movement and coordination. One of the many symptoms of this condition includes difficulty with visual-spatial awareness which can result in issues navigating where you are without walking into things, dropping things, or knocking things over. Following the diagnosis, I still considered myself clumsy and stupid and I judged my body constantly: from not being good at sport to not feeling I could wear shorts or skirts due to my legs being covered in bruises. I struggled to regard my body with any respect, and I would consistently push it to its limit.

As I headed down the slippery path to burnout and overwhelm, I increasingly resented my body for beginning to carry tiredness and pain – and as time went on, I found it was unable to do what I needed it to do. Feeling exhausted all day, my mind would spring to life at night, so sleep would feel out of reach, and my weakened immune system was like a sponge to every bug going around.

There wasn't a defining moment when my body switched from wellness to illness – I just didn't know how to listen to the warning signs it was giving me along the way.

Your body is like an incredible and sophisticated machine: your skin provides protection, your skeleton and muscles give it a structural foundation, your organs provide the most remarkable functions to keep you alive, and your sensory system is feeding information so you know when to react, or not. If you were a car, you would be having a regular MOT and service to make sure you were roadworthy and reliable!

You may well already be considering your health and well-being by eating a good diet and doing regular exercise, which is great – but what are you doing about the daily stresses which may already be chipping away at your physical health?

The combining function of the brain and body

We often look at our brain and body as two very separate entities, yet they are inextricably linked, one impacting the other. They work on a feedback loop, so the way you think influences how you feel, and vice versa. Both are communicating all the time and the messages they send allow the brain and body to adjust its response. For instance, if an unexpected football is hurtling through the air towards you, you are going to duck! If your body is thirsty, a message to the brain would send you looking for a drink.

We use phrases regularly to describe a mind-body experience, such as 'he's a pain in the neck', and 'she made my blood boil', or even 'I had a gut feeling'. Difficult situations which induce a feeling of vulnerability might mean you draw your shoulders forwards to protect your heart. When feeling nervous, you may have an uneasy feeling in your abdomen. With anger your heart rate will speed up and your body temperature will increase like hot lava rushing to your head. If anger is unexpressed it can result in hands drawn into fists, tension in the jaw and a tightening of muscles in the arms, shoulders, back of the neck, and head.

As a child you may not have been taught how to deal with uncomfortable feelings so you may have locked them into your body, carrying them into adulthood where you continue to add to them, moment-by-moment. This can put a strain on the body so it will begin to communicate its stress via regular headaches, colds, pain, or even digestive complaints. But really, the systems of the body are switching on the warning lights of stress.

Often the gut is referred to as the *second brain* or the *little brain* because of its nerve connections to the brain. It is certainly affected by fight-or-flight, and from an evolutionary point of view, it would have been necessary for us to have an empty bowel and bladder to flee from threats. We often use the term 'upset tummy' to describe a digestive complaint, but it can in fact be the result of nerves, whilst churning can be the result of worry.

The stress hormones adrenaline and cortisol, produced during fight-or-flight, are secreted into the body to give it enough energy to get away from any perceived threat. However, when these hormones are released regularly, the body diverts its attention more to the threat rather than bringing awareness to any infections which could be in the body, which is why stress can bring an increase of coughs and colds. In other words, the body is focused on surviving, rather than thriving.

In previous chapters we have seen how the relaxation response can counterbalance stress to help with digestive issues and coughs and colds, but what about the pain of headaches and migraines – both of which can also be triggered by emotional or physical stress?

What happens when we feel pain or discomfort?

None of us want to experience pain, but it can often be caused by stress, illness, injury, or damage to the body. Acute pain usually passes within six months, whilst chronic pain is ongoing and generally lasts longer than six months. Our brain will work out how it wants to react to pain, and a natural reaction is to push it away. We will tense up our mind and body as our brain processes the pain information. Our brain also adds an emotional response to the pain – in fact, many emotions attach themselves to pain, which can serve to intensify the feeling. This is often referred to as 'secondary suffering' and describes how a cycle of pain and emotions are interconnected.

There have been many scientific studies which have demonstrated how meditation can help reduce pain or even help you to manage it better. This is because there is less activity in the part of the brain which is associated with processing pain, and increased activity in the areas associated with emotional processing. This means people who meditate are less likely to have a heightened reaction to pain.

When I began my meditation practice, my awareness of the link between the body and mind grew and, during the stillness of the practice, I began to listen to how my body would communicate with me. The practice gave me the space to view what was happening and the stories I was telling myself about my body, so I was better able to choose how to respond. This meant I was less likely to pin a fearful thought or feeling to the experience, and instead view it with equanimity. In fact, it helped me to accept my body so I could feel more at home within it. Nowadays, I view my dyspraxia with care, regard, and even humour.

Body scan

The body scan meditation focuses your attention on the sensations in each part of your body. It is an opportunity to bring your mind and body to oneness, so that you can view, with awareness, what is taking place.

During the meditation there may be an urge to judge and create stories about your body: if there is a part of your body which you don't like or which currently holds pain or discomfort, your mind will naturally want to analyse or overthink it. In the body scan you will begin to become aware of when you are adding stories to your experience. For instance, if you have pain or discomfort in your back you may recall times when it has affected your work or sleep. This may bring up feelings such as irritability or discomfort. But through this meditation we learn to 'be' with the sensations as they are, without trying to change or create stories about them. Instead, we realise we can choose our response, as well as recognise the impermanence of each moment. We can do this by viewing our body in a curious and interested way.

Let's meditate: body scan

Listen to this audio meditation at sarahepresley.co.uk/making-friends-with-yourself/meditations

This meditation is all about coming home to your body, by bringing a oneness to your body and mind. You will be noticing the sensations of your body, in a non-judgemental way, so you can learn to be with your body in its natural state. This is regardless of whether the sensation is pleasant, unpleasant, or even neutral – you will be noticing what is there.

You may want to set a tone to view your body in a curious and interested way. This will allow you to have a mindful experience with the

body scan, so you are just being present with whatever is there.

Be aware of your breath coming in and out of your body . . . . No need to change your breath, simply be aware of your breath as it is . . . . Feel it coming into your body and back out again . . . .

With awareness still on your breath, notice the surface upon which your body is currently resting. Allow yourself to be held by the surface, so you can relax. If there is an area of discomfort, you can always bring the breath there.

As you continue to place your attention on your breath, imagine your breath is like a spotlight coming in and out of your body. This spotlight may be shining awareness at your nose, perhaps the tip . . . . Or you might be aware of the sensation of breath going up through your nostrils and back out again . . . . Or the spotlight of breath may take the journey through the nostrils, through the throat and into the chest before you exhale and release . . . . Or perhaps the spotlight of breath may be at your lungs, noticing how they inflate and deflate . . . . Or maybe you notice your breath at your abdomen, aware of the belly rising as you breathe in and going back towards your spine as you breathe out . . . .

Now, imagine the breath spotlight taking a journey through your body. Be aware as it now goes to your pelvis and legs until it reaches your feet and toes.

Resting the spotlight of your attention at your toes, notice them as they are without changing them in any way. Maybe you are aware of the temperature, the bones, the skin. Noticing, without judging or reacting . . . .

Your mind might be giving you many reasons not to focus on your toes right now, and that's OK. You can let go of any thoughts you have and gently come back to your toes . . . . before resting your awareness at your feet.

As you notice them, you might be aware of your socks or shoes or the surface your feet are resting on. Your feet carry you around all day, so be with the sensation, whatever is there . . . .

Now shine the spotlight of your mind's eye onto the tops of your feet . . . . Then move to your ankles before resting your attention on your calves and shins. Are the sensations constant, or do they change? Being aware of this, without any judgement. Just pure awareness . . . .

Now move your awareness to your knees . . . noticing your knees as they are. You may feel stiffness or discomfort . . . hold this awareness with softness and interest . . . .

And now rest the spotlight of awareness on your thighs. Maybe you can feel your clothes against your skin, or you might be aware of your muscles. Be at home in your body, as it is – not changing it, but being with it in this moment . . . .

Now, allow your awareness to rest on your pelvis. Notice your buttocks and your hips: one hip, and then the other. What sensations are you aware of now? You might notice tightness or pressure, or you may not be feeling any sensations. There is no right or wrong way to experience your body. So, if you are not aware of any sensations right now, that is OK . . . .

Next, bring the spotlight to your abdomen: sometimes we hold tension here and you may be aware of this now. You may even find your mind is wandering and creating stories about your experience. It's OK. When you realise, gently come back to noticing your abdomen and the sensations: being with the sensations . . . being with this moment . . . .

And now bring your awareness up to your chest. Perhaps you notice your ribcage or your lungs or the muscles on your chest wall. Rest your attention on this area. Be in the direct experience. Not changing it but accepting what is there . . . .

Now bring your attention to your lower back . . . . Next, extend your awareness to include the middle of your back . . . . and now include the top of your back . . . You might notice your shoulder blades or your spine. Perhaps there is tightness, stiffness or even discomfort. You may even find you are judging your body. Gently let go of the judgement, and come back to the soft and interested part of your mind. Recognise what is here in this moment . . . .

Take the spotlight now down your arms: starting at the tops of your arms . . . . then move to your elbows . . . your forearms . . . . your wrists . . . . the tops of your hands . . . . your palms . . . . and then your fingers and thumbs all the way to the tips

. . . . Bring pure awareness to the entirety of your arms all the way from the top to the tips of your fingers and thumbs . . . . Notice what is there.

Now go back to the tops of your arms, but this time rest your awareness at your shoulders . . . . We're not trying to change what is here but holding it with a soft interest . . . .

Next, bring the spotlight to your throat and neck . . . . What is happening at your neck? Are there any sore spots or feelings of discomfort? Now take your awareness up to the back of your head and the curve of your skull and be with the direct sensation here . . . . Notice if your mind is creating a dialogue, and then gently bringing your awareness to the back of your head before resting your attention on your jaw . . . . Feel your jaw – is it tense or loose? What about your mouth? Your tongue? Your lips? Now notice your cheeks . . . . and then your nose . . . Now bring your awareness to your eyes . . . . and then the area around your eyes . . . . and your eyelids . . . . then notice your forehead – just as it is . . . . notice your temples . . . . notice your ears . . . . and then the sides of your head above your ears . . . .

And then bring the spotlight to the top of your head . . . .

Now return your focus to your breath coming in and out of your body.

Notice your breath at your nose. The surface beneath your feet.

And when you are ready, and in your own time, gently open your eyes.

Body-mind connection in a purposeful way

Were you creating stories about different aspects of your body? The very fact you have noticed is key. The more you can bring awareness, the more you can begin to choose your response. Rather than getting caught up within the stress of the story, you will be much more able to see things 'as is' – not only in your body, but in the outer world too.

Everyday activities can be a way of noticing your body-mind connection: just by engaging your senses you are able to view your emotional/thought reaction. How about we try this with the act of washing your hands?

Let's be mindful: washing hands

Turn on the tap and be aware of the temperature of the tap against your skin – is the flow of water slow or fast?

Now place your hands under the flow – does the temperature feel OK for you? Is it too cold, too hot, or just right? Do you want to change the temperature to suit you better?

With the water running on your hands, are you aware of any splashes of water which reach other parts of your body or clothes? What thoughts or feelings does this bring for you? What about the sound of the water? Does the sound become different depending on where you hold your hands in the water? What about the sound of the water against the sink?

Now reach for the soap – can you smell the soap already? How far away does the soap have to be from your nose before you can smell it? Does the smell remind you of anything? Be aware of its colour and the texture. Is the colour a good match for the smell? What about the sensation of the soap as you move it around your hands? How does it feel on your hands? Do the sensations change as you move it around?

Continue to clean your hands with awareness and notice how your hands move in synchronisation with each other. Each hand knows how it needs to support the other through the process of washing hands, so be aware of how they move instinctively together. Witness how your fingers and thumbs move. Notice your skin and your fingernails.

As you wash off the soap, notice the suds making their journey down the plug hole. Turn off the tap with awareness and then notice the sensations of the towel as you dry your hands.

This exercise can be applied to any daily experience, from brushing your teeth, to making the bed, to eating a meal. Living in a purposeful way does not mean you have to create perfectly beautiful moments. Instead, it opens up the opportunity to view ourselves and learn how we interact with the outside world. It may even reconnect you with the simpler things in life.

I used to feel resentful about washing and drying up following a meal. When seeing the build-up of plates and cups I would generate stories about how I felt all the household jobs were left for me. So, I decided to use the drying up as a mindfulness experience.

Through mindfully picking up the cutlery from the draining board, I felt the cool of the metal against my hands. I looked at my distorted reflection in the handles and the spoon, and examined the shape and design. As I did this, I was reminded of the generosity of someone who had bought it for me many years before. I recognised how she must have stood in the shop, looking at many different designs. I realised how much I liked the design and how well the cutlery had served me, my family and friends over the years. To bring myself back to the present, I picked up a plate and immediately noticed a chip on the edge. I felt a rise of judgment, as the chip reminded me of being dyspraxic and the daily difficulty in navigating the dishes back into the cupboards. As I let go of this story, I also recalled the day my husband and I had chosen the set due to its sturdiness and the lovely colour. I continued to move from object to object, observing and examining with my senses along the way, and found myself experiencing a joyful feeling as I did so. Since then, the task of washing and drying-up the dishes feels different, and has made me feel much more appreciative of the things I took for granted before.

*

In this chapter we have explored our body by engaging our senses. We have witnessed how this allows us to view our response to what is happening in the moment and help us to develop our mindfulness experience in a non-judgemental way.

Let's now take the next step to inner calm, exploring why we can feel consumed with worry and how meditation can help.

Chapter Seven:

Making Friends With Your Worries

Understanding your relationship with worry

Worries used to create movies within my mind of epic proportions: if Steven Spielberg had taken a peek inside my head, he would most certainly be attempting to buy the movie rights!

Whilst you were not born into the world as a worrier, as you have grown into adulthood, your everyday concerns may have become a prominent feature in your personal world. As a child you may not have been taught what to do with worries. Now you are an adult, on a daily basis, you may feel you are carrying their weight on your shoulders – or you might even be aware of your worries churning in the pit of your stomach.

I came from a long line of worriers, including my mum and my grandmother. I can recall being proud of my worries, even referring to myself as 'the born worrier' – in fact, if there wasn't anything to feel worried about, I would feel uneasy.

There were two reasons I worried. The first was because I cared – as a small child I had learnt this from my Nan when I asked her, 'Nan, why do you worry about everyone?', and she replied, 'Because I care'. It was immediately apparent to me she cared deeply about those she loved and so it was only natural to be concerned about them too.

The second reason came when I realised life didn't always turn out the way I had expected it to. I couldn't trust the flow of life and I felt a lack of control over situations and the people around me.

So simply put, we worry because we feel fearful about the people and things we care about. And falsely, we believe our worries will help us to feel in control of our fear.

Why worry?

Throughout this book we have been learning about the incredible inbuilt system we have within our body which assesses situations for danger – if it perceives there is a threat, it will act accordingly. A little bit of worry can be helpful to motivate us to complete a task, but interestingly, our brain cannot discern between fact or fiction. If you are worrying about something which isn't happening in the here and now, your brain will still act accordingly and will potentially place you in another fight-or-flight response, even if there is no need to be. For instance, if you are thinking about a new project you are about to start but feel apprehensive, your brain will notice the feeling of vulnerability assume there is a threat in front of you right now, and cut off communication with the prefrontal lobe, which houses our rational thinking.

Excessive worrying can be destructive and demonstrates how difficult it is to trust the process of life to unfold in a balanced way. Perhaps there has been a major situation, or a number of minor situations which have affected your trust, and you falsely believe that you can protect yourself by worrying about the things you can't control. With the breakdown in communication between the amygdala (the emotional control centre) and the rational part of the brain, it will be difficult to see a solution to the worry so your brain will sit within the fear, thus creating fictional stories.

Worry is fiction.

When you are worrying, you are not living: you are removed from the outside world, analysing and obsessing over situations which have either happened or have not happened yet, as the pull of uncertainty is too strong to ignore. However, being inside your head means you deny yourself the right to witness the other moments of beauty unfolding around you.

Worrying doesn't bring solutions and is not conducive to happiness. In fact, it is unpleasant and can impact your energy. If anyone worries about me, I don't feel grateful to them for spending time and energy on my problems. Instead, I feel they lack trust and faith in me to resolve my own issues.

How do you stop the worries?

Life doesn't come with a toolkit on how to deal with worries. When you were young and expressing your worries, you might have been told 'don't worry' – with good intentions and reassurance. But in many ways, your discomfort may have been making the other person feel uncomfortable because they hadn't learnt to deal with their own worries.

Worries may not change overnight, but it is possible to reframe the way you think about worries. This is where meditation comes in handy – we have already learnt how meditation creates the perfect counterbalance to fight-or-flight, plus it can give you the space to be the observer and decide how you want to respond. In this chapter, we are also going to look at some additional meditation techniques we can use in our toolkit, but first, we are going to explore guided visualisation.

Introducing guided visualisation meditation

In some ways the name of this type of meditation can be slightly misleading, and I feel a better name would be 'guided experience'. The word 'visualisation' leads to the impression you are only going to be picturing something in your mind. And yet, these types of meditations are more than that.

You may create a picture within your mind, but you can also engage all of your senses. The meditation app, Headspace, describe it as a 'focused practice that involves each of the five senses to ignite positive healing messages throughout the mind and body'. If I were to ask you to describe a beach, you might close your eyes and start telling me about the colour of the sky, the warm sand beneath your feet and the sound of the waves on the shore. In this moment, your mind was using your own personal experience of beaches to create this mental representation, it just may be that one part of your senses is stronger than another.

It is also important to understand that one in fifty people are unable to visualise – what's known as aphantasia. I am the one in fifty, yet I find these meditations hugely beneficial – as I listen to the guidance I 'feel' the experience taking place rather than picturing it, but you may find one of your other senses can be engaged instead. Ed Catmull, former president of Pixar and Walt Disney Animations, also has aphantasia. After doing a survey of his former employees, he was surprised to learn some of the world's best animators have it, which shows us that not being able to 'picture' will not affect your ability to be creative.

Research has shown these types of meditation will promote relaxation, reduce stress and anxiety, and ease various symptoms relating to stress. In David Hamilton PhD's book *How Your Mind Can Heal Your Body*, he explores the power of visualisation, belief, positive thinking and their effects on the body. Top athletes have been known to use this technique to help them get the best out of their performance too.

As we learnt earlier, the body cannot always discern between what is happening now and what has happened in the past. That means that for guided visualisations, the mental representations you create with your senses will feel real to your body. For instance, if you create the sense of watching waves lapping on the shore of a beach right now, you may find you experience the same feeling of peacefulness or relaxation you have felt when experiencing it in real life.

In addition to this, you can use your imagination to help you to let go of your worries. For instance, you could place the word 'worry' onto an imaginary cloud and watch or sense it passing by until it disappears. With this technique you are learning to let go of your worries.

Letting go of the worry *doesn't* mean you don't care. Instead, it means you are creating more space between what is happening and what you are worried about happening, allowing your body the opportunity to connect with the calmer part of yourself and the rationale part of the mind to engage with possible solutions.

Let's meditate: letting go meditation

Listen to this audio meditation at sarahpresley.co.uk/making-friends-with-yourself/meditations

Close your eyes, or place your gaze on a non-moving spot in the room. Feel yourself being held

by the surface beneath you, so you can rest in your experience. Begin by bringing your awareness to your breath coming in and out of your body, and when you feel ready take three deep breaths in your own time . . . .

Imagine your breath can relax every part of your body, so you can feel your body beginning to relax from the top of your head, down to the tip of your toes . . . . Relaxing and releasing each time you breathe . . . . as you bring the relaxation to the muscles in the top of your head . . . . the back of your head . . . . your face . . . . now your neck . . . . your throat, as you become more and more relaxed, and more and more comfortable . . . . Now bringing the relaxation to your shoulders, feel the muscles beginning to release . . . . the tops of your arms . . . . forearms, hands, fingers and thumbs . . . . now the top of your back. . . the middle of your back . . . . and the bottom of your back, as you become more and more relaxed, and more and more comfortable . . . . Now bringing the relaxing breath down to your chest . . . . your abdomen . . . . now relaxing the muscles of your pelvis, your hips and your buttocks . . . . thighs, knees, shins and calves, feet and toes, as you become more and more relaxed, and more and more comfortable.

If your mind wanders, bring it back to your breath and the relaxing of your body.

Now imagine, pretend, or get a sense that you are standing in front of a beautiful still lake – the lake is a body of water, held in the earth's embrace . . . . Perhaps your lake is reflecting all that is around it – maybe your lake is surrounded by plants or trees. Or it may be surrounded by mountains or a vast open space. Perhaps your lake is reflecting the sun and the clouds in the sky. Or perhaps it is a night-time sky reflecting the moon and the stars . . . . Don't worry if you are unable to get an exact image. Whatever the image or feeling of your lake, just breathe with the stillness . . . .

In your pocket is a pebble and as you take it out, you notice it has the word 'worry' written on it. Feel the weight of the pebble and acknowledge any thoughts or feelings which come to mind . . . .

Then, when you are ready, throw the pebble into the lake and notice as it splashes into the lake before reaching the sand at the bottom. The splash sends a cascade of ripples which spread out across the lake . . . . before once again the lake becomes still . . . .

You have let go of your worries, and you are free. You are free to fill your mind with happier thoughts that all is well. In this moment, there is no past, no future and you can just be . . . .

Be aware of the stillness of the lake and bring the stillness into your body and mind . . . . You can feel at one with the stillness . . . .

Now bring awareness to your breath at your nose, and your feet resting on the surface they are on. And gently open your eyes.

Well done! You have made your first steps towards learning how to let go of your worries. You have given yourself the opportunity to create space for your body and mind to react with calmness.

Other techniques for letting go of worries

In chapter three we looked at neuroplasticity and how experience can change the brain, so with consistent practice you can learn to let go of your worries. To do this, you first need to identify and bring awareness to the fact that you are worrying. Once you have done this, you can use any of the following techniques:

1. Get creative with your own guided visualisation. Think of things which create the feeling of space between you and the worry. Perhaps you could imagine placing your worries on a leaf as it drifts down a stream, or placing your worries onto an aeroplane and watching it fly away until you can't see it anymore. You can really get creative and have fun with this.
2. Label the worry. You could identify where you feel the worry in your body – it may be a churning feeling in your abdomen – and then label it as 'worry' and breathe the feeling out from your abdomen.
3. Give your worry a happy ending in your mind. How many of your worries have actually come true? It's your own movie in your mind – what happens if you decide to imagine a solution instead?

All of these techniques can help you to retrain your mind so that your fears no longer consume or define you. And whilst it might not change overnight, it will be the consequence of a repetitive practice. Life is always going to have ups and downs and twists and turns, but through the consistency of these practices you will be more willing to go with the flow and see where it takes you. You will have measured the risk and feel much happier taking a chance with the unknown.

As we are learning, we will not be able to switch off our thoughts when we are meditating, and at times they can create quite a distraction. In the next chapter we are going to look at putting down positive foundations in how we deal with our thoughts when they interrupt our practice.

Chapter Eight:

Meditation Foundation: Thoughts

Your thoughts are your friends

'We simply recognise it's a thought, it's not who I really am. By its very nature a thought, however intense, is impermanent; it is visiting, it is arising due to conditioning or habit. Very gently let it go. Bring your attention back, one breath at a time'. These words written by Sharon Salzberg in her book, *Real Happiness: The Power of Meditation*, flew off the page and struck me hard in the centre of my heart. Within my meditation practice I had already learnt how to let go of most of my thoughts, but at times I could be distracted by those which focused on what was wrong with my life – I still couldn't always switch off from the destructive self-talk. The wisdom of her words was important for me to hear and I felt instant relief in the knowledge that I could treat each thought as a visitor and not always feel I had to act on them.

Buddhists often refer to our thinking mind as a wild monkey which swings from stories to fantasies to dramas. Unable to sit still for long, the monkey mind is often restless, inconsistent, and uncontrollable.

Does this sound familiar?

Most of us can often feel out of control as we swirl from one thought to the next, and so on. This is due to our brain constantly gathering information from the stimuli around us via our sensory system. It does this to keep us safe – its main job is to alert us to possible threats and dangers.

Most thoughts will be mundane and form the chitter-chatter backdrop to your everyday life, such as: 'the sky is a light grey today', or 'I can feel a slight breeze', or 'my toothpaste is minty'. These types of thought do not spell danger and so there will be no reason to form an attachment to them. Other thoughts can be positive ones, such as 'oh, I can smell jasmine! It reminds me of Pete and Jackie's wedding, such a beautiful day. I wish we were still there'. With these types of thoughts, you may want to savour the memory of them yet also be fearful of what is behind them if you let them go, in which case an attachment might be made. Negative thoughts will drop in and hook into your psyche, creating questions in an ever-increasing circle: 'there's an empty coffee cup left on the side – why doesn't anyone ever clean up after themselves? Why is it always me who does everything around here? No one ever does anything for me.'

It is the attachment to the thought which often creates a problem, and this is summed up in this well-known quote by Lao Tzu; 'If you are depressed you are living in the past. If you anxious you are living in the future. If you are at peace you are living in the present'. This isn't to make light of mental health issues, but instead to demonstrate how an attachment to our thoughts can bring out strong emotions.

Distractions happen

When my children were young, I would announce to them and my husband, 'I am going to meditate,' and I would shut the door to our spare room where I had set up some comfy cushions. Of course, I had an expectation everyone would put their lives on hold whilst I took some quiet time for myself. Yet the sounds of my children playing and shouting outside was my reality, along with the loud music being played by my husband in the kitchen. During some practices, I might also be distracted by the aroma of food being prepared for our evening meal, or the temperature of the room would be too cold. Then there would be the times when I found it hard to relax as my clothes would feel uncomfortable against my skin.

Sometimes when meditating, you'll be unable to press pause on the world. It will feel as if the volume has been turned up as you become much more aware of your body, thoughts, feelings, and environment. Discomfort, which is usually quietly acknowledged, will interfere with your flow. The sounds which normally form the backdrop to your experience will suddenly feel intrusive. Or there could even be an unacknowledged emotion from earlier in the day which has laid dormant under the surface but chooses to rise in a quiet moment.

Whilst you will allow most of these distractions to pass on by, it will be inevitable some will hang around. The key moment is when you notice you are attached to the distraction – even if a few minutes have gone by – and then, without judging, you gently return to your focused awareness.

In chapter six, we experienced a mindfulness practice known as the body scan, but we can use similar mindfulness techniques to view the distractions and see how we are creating stories about our experience. Mark Williams in *Mindfulness: A Practical Guide to Finding Peace in a Frantic World* says, 'You can't stop the triggering of unhappy memories, self-critical thoughts, and judgmental ways of thinking – but you can stop what happens next. You can stop the spiral from feeding off itself and triggering the next cycle of negative thoughts. You can stop the cascade of destructive emotions that can end up making you unhappy, anxious, stressed, irritable or exhausted.'

This is where a mindfulness exercise called 'Labelling the thoughts' can be a handy tool for giving you enough space to consider your response.

Labelling the thought

If a thought is distracting, you can give it a label. For instance, you could label the thought as 'thinking'. The moment you give the thought a label you immediately become the observer of the thought, and you can choose whether you want to hold onto it or let it go. Alternatively, you can label the type of thought you have – so if you are thinking 'I must get some bananas tomorrow', you could label this as 'remembering'. If you are thinking about a project at work, you could label it as 'planning'. Or if you are ruminating about a discussion with your partner, you could label it as 'ruminating'. It isn't about finding the perfect label, though – if the only word which comes to mind is 'jam', it's OK. You can use any word to acknowledge the distraction.

You can also label emotions. A functional MRI scan study (which measures the small changes in blood flow that occur with brain activity) by Matt Lieberman at UCLA showed labelling the emotion in this way appears to decrease activity in the brain's emotional centres, including the amygdala. As author Dan Siegel says, you 'name it to tame it'.

Shall we give it a go?

Let's meditate: labelling thoughts meditation

Listen to this audio meditation at sarahpresley.co.uk/making-friends-with-yourself/meditations

Be aware of your body making contact with the surface it is on. Allow yourself to be held so you can rest in your experience . . . .

When you feel ready, gently close your eyes, or place your eyes on a fixed spot in the room . . . .

You may be aware of the sounds around you, the temperature, or smells. Allow them to be there without judging.

Now rest your attention on your breath as it comes in and out of your body . . . . You can focus your attention wherever you want in your body: perhaps feeling the sensation of your breath on your upper lip or on the tip of your nose . . . . Or you might notice the movement of your breath taking its journey through your nostrils, or into your lungs . . . . You might notice your lungs expanding or deflating, or you may be more aware of the muscle movements in your chest wall or your abdomen . . . . If you prefer, you could always label your breath, 'Aware of my breath coming in, aware of my breath going out' . . . . Just allow yourself to get behind one breath at a time, feeling the rhythm of the breath coming in and going back out . . . .

It won't be long before you start to notice yourself becoming distracted. Your mind will wander away from your breath: remembering, daydreaming, or worrying. This is not a sign to say you can't meditate, but the nature of the current moment and so when you realise you have been distracted, you could always give it a label: 'Thinking', and then come back to your breath:

'Aware of my breath coming in, aware of my breath going out' . . . .

It is a bit like staring at a beautiful blue sky and watching the clouds go by. Your mind is the blue sky, and your thoughts are like the white clouds. They are the visitors, and you are the observer . . . .

If you find yourself on the cloud with the thought, label it as 'thinking' and return to the focus of your breath: 'aware of my breath coming in, aware of my breath going out' . . . .

Feeling present in this moment – allowing the moment to be as it is . . . .

Noticing how each moment arises, develops, and passes on by . . . .

And remembering: a thought is just a thought; it's not who you are, it's just visiting. So, label it as 'thinking' and return to your breath: 'aware of my breath coming in, aware of my breath going out' . . . .

And now be aware of your body resting on your chair, feeling the support. Your breath at your nose. And gently open your eyes.

You are not your thoughts

Some people find they don't need to use the labelling process and can easily let go of their thoughts and return to their breath. But for others, it can be a useful tool.

I often use this technique when I am walking my dog, especially if my mind is twisting and turning around various dramatic scenarios in my life. Every time I realise my mind has become distracted, I label it as 'thinking' and then bring my attention back to either the sound of my feet on the pavement or watching my dog's ears flapping as she trots beside me. The more I repeat this, the more my mind can calm, and I can enjoy the time with my dog as well as being aware of my surroundings.

But what about the sound triggers?

Our perception of sound when we are meditating is impacted by our personal life experience and perceptions. A barking dog can be incredibly annoying for some, whilst for others it might bring about concern for the welfare of the dog. The click of a washing machine finishing its cycle may initially be a reminder to remove the laundry but can bring a chain of thoughts and frustrations about all the chores to be done around the house. A neighbour slamming his car door may be a reminder of other inconsiderate behaviour he has displayed previously. Before you know it, a whole movie has played out inside your head!

Backdrop to the meditation experience

If we accept sounds exist, we can see that they form the backdrop to our meditation practice. We can recognise when we have been distracted by them, acknowledge and then let go. This helps us to welcome the sounds and make friends with them.

My work room is very quiet, and I might occasionally hear the sound of a barking dog, or a faint hum of traffic, but mostly I can hear the birds tweeting outside. On one occasion when a client had come for a relaxing treatment, my neighbour's house alarm began to ring shrilly. Knowing it might do so for some time, I said to my client: 'we have two choices here. You can either go home and we arrange for you to come back here another time, or you can welcome the sound as part of your experience today – you could allow the sound to simply exist'. Within five minutes she was asleep, and at the end of the treatment she was astounded at how she could sleep through such noise.

When you accept the sounds, it can give your meditation practice a better flow. However, there may still be occasions when you get carried away with thoughts about the sound, so you can create a mindfulness experience with this, too.

Let's meditate: awareness of sound meditation

Listen to this audio meditation at sarahpresley.co.uk/making-friends-with-yourself/meditations

Either close your eyes or keep them open and on a fixed spot. Be aware of the space you occupy and notice your body and the surface it is on . . . . Allow the surface to hold you, so you can rest in your experience . . . .

Gently bring awareness to your breath coming in and out of your body . . . .

Whilst you are with your breath, extend your awareness to include the sounds around you too . . . . There are sounds outside of your room . . . . sounds inside your room . . . . and sounds inside your body . . . . The sounds may be constant or intermittent . . . . notice how some sounds arise, develop, and then pass on by . . . .

If your mind is creating stories about the sounds, you can label as 'hear' and then return to your breath . . . .

So, you are being with your breath, but noticing the sounds around you . . . . You may be aware of the tone, the pitch or even the duration of the sound . . . . Some sounds may be loud, some may be soft . . . .

If you are feeling distracted by the sound, label as 'hear' and come back to being the observer of your breath and the sounds rather than being the participant . . . .

In some moments you may need to label 'hear' quite often and in other moments you will find it easy to be with your breath and the sounds around you . . . . There is no need to judge if you are feeling distracted, this is just the nature of the moment you are in . . . . Wherever you are, whatever happens you can always come back to your breath . . . .

Now bring your attention again to the surface you are resting on, feeling your body being held. Notice your breath at your nose. And then gently open your eyes.

Thoughts, feelings, and the environment around us are going to create distractions to our practice – but how we treat them is important. We can tense up our body and mind, or we can treat them like a friend and recognise they are impermanent and just part of our meditation experience. Meditation isn't escapism, but instead offers us an opportunity to observe, giving us much more power to choose how and when we respond.

But what happens if we find ourselves overcome with feelings of anger? In the next chapter we are going to look at why we feel angry and how meditation can help.

Chapter Nine:

Making Friends With Anger

Understanding your relationship with anger

I used to tell people I wasn't an angry person, yet this wasn't true. Whilst I might not have been displaying much anger outwardly, I would be quietly seething inside. Inevitably, the anger would simmer away – sometimes for months on end – until it reached boiling point, eventually discharging itself in an explosive rage. I would initially feel relief from the release, but in the aftermath, I would feel an immense sense of shame and guilt and judge myself to be a dreadful human being.

I contained my anger on the inside as I was worried I wouldn't be liked by others – I only wanted them to see the 'good' side of me. Rather than confronting the negative and destructive behaviour of friends and colleagues, I would choose a spiral of inner blame instead. I would be the first to apologise for situations which were not my fault – even if someone stood on my toe I would be the one saying 'sorry'! This built up more internal loathing, yet I would continue to present an exterior of being calm and happy.

Why do we react?

Stimuli around us create an emotional response, which can range from the negative, such as sadness or rage, to the positive, such as joy and happiness – and everything else in between.

These emotions provide the motivation to act when necessary, as well as helping us to understand ourselves and others much better. Anger comes from the limbic part of the brain and is normally developed between two and six months of age, when it helps us to alert our carers to the danger we feel we are in – which at this age may quite simply be an uncomfortable dirty nappy or a hungry tummy.

Anger is a primitive response, one which is also shared by animals. In primal times, our anger would have allowed us to fight or escape from the saber-toothed tiger, but in modern times it comes as we interpret psychological triggers. This can be different for each of us, as past and current circumstances will have an impact on how you react.

If you were to examine the root of your anger you would recognise it comes from situations in which you have felt vulnerable – this may be due to feeling under threat or attack, moments when you have felt powerless, situations where you felt you were judged unfairly, or times when your feelings have not seemed important to another person. For some, it can be feeling there is too much pressure from the responsibilities of life.

Just like with worries, you may not have been given the toolkit for dealing with anger, so you may have found it difficult to manage your feelings, resulting in angry outbursts. Or you may have been chastised for your emotions and instead learnt to contain your anger. Some may have learnt to use their anger to get their own way.

Understanding your own anger

If you were to stand back and observe your anger, you would see that it reflects something within you which needs attention. Do you honour your own feelings before letting them go? Or do the people and situations which ignite your anger actually reflect aspects of yourself you would rather not see?

Anger, like any emotion, is a message to let you know how you are feeling in a particular situation. It isn't wrong to feel angry – it's what you choose to do with the emotion which is key. If it isn't expressed in a healthy way, it will have an impact on your mental and physical health, and affect the relationships around you.

Allowing yourself to see the root of your anger is the first step to breaking the cycle. We often think our anger is a sudden and uncontrollable explosion, but if we were to examine its path, we may find it can come from a build-up over time –

perhaps stemming from the moments when we didn't address our own needs in a vulnerable moment. For instance, you may have a partner who gives you a little peck on your cheek before leaving for work every morning – but one day, they leave the room without the usual kiss. Expecting them to realise their error and return, you are shocked when you hear the click of the front door shutting behind them. You may instantly feel confused or even concerned about the sudden change in behaviour, leading you to feel discomfort and vulnerability as you wonder what has changed for your partner to behave in this way. Perhaps your mind begins to play out stories – in some scenarios you blame yourself for their actions, and in others you are fearful something has happened to them to warrant the change. Or you may push the feelings to one side, telling yourself you are silly for being so concerned. Without dealing with the uncomfortable feelings, you may find that as the day continues your senses become heightened to further danger. Later, as you drive to an appointment, a car suddenly pulls out in front of you, and this allows you to finally let out the full charge of angry energy which has resided within you all day, and so you press hard on your car horn and shout every expletive you know at a complete stranger.

The anger in others can also contribute to our feelings of vulnerability. When my youngest son was of primary school age, I was watching him at football practice and I witnessed his joy when one of his coaches praised his football skills. Within moments, another boy ran over to my son and angrily screamed in his face. The joy fell from him as I watched his expression change from shock, to confusion, and then to sadness. For the rest of the practice, his head and shoulders slumped down and he seemed to have lost any enthusiasm for playing football. On the journey home, I raised the issue and he told me he felt sad as he didn't know what he had done to deserve such behaviour. I explained that we may never understand what makes another person angry, however we can instead view the anger as a burning piece of coal the boy had been carrying and which was most likely hurting him inside. By screaming at my son he had found a way to get rid of it, yet by accepting his behaviour it was now my son who was carrying the burning coal. I said to him, 'What do you want to do with the burning coal?' and he replied, 'I don't want to throw it back to the boy as it will only hurt him again. I also don't want to throw it at you, as it will hurt you. But if I hold onto the coal, it will continue to hurt me. Instead, I am going to breathe it out from my body and imagine it is going into a bucket of cold water.'

As you can see, we created space to observe the vulnerability and take care of the emotions which were raised. We also felt compassion for the other person. However, it takes practice to sit with what you are feeling in a calm and compassionate way. This is why meditation can be a step in the right direction.

Respect for your emotions = respect for yourself

Meditation allows us to practice the techniques of being with emotions in a safe way. For instance, during a meditation session, there can be moments when it is hard to be in the constant state of flow so it would be easy to feel the rise of frustration within your mind and body. If someone is making a sound in the room next to you, you might feel inconsequential, perhaps leading to feelings of sadness or disappointment. Or there may be an unexpressed emotion which has been sat under the surface all day which decides to make its presence known to you when you sit down to meditate.

Often, we will try and push our feelings away, but the more we push, the more our bodies will tense against it and the stronger the emotion will become. Instead of pushing it away, we can give the strong emotion a moment of our attention and embrace it as part of our current meditation experience. This will help us to accept the feeling, and through acceptance, we will realise we have three choices: do you want to stay in the chaos of the anger and sit inside the stories about why you feel the way you do; do you want to lean into the emotion for a moment and allow it to be; or do you want to let it go?

To let it go, we can once again return to the labelling technique – so if you feel frustration within your meditation experience you could label it as 'frustration' and breathe it out. You could even locate the feeling within your body and allow it to leave on your breath.

When you do this, you are honouring your emotions – and yourself – by recognising that the feeling exists rather than pushing it away or feeling that you shouldn't have it. For a moment, you are giving the emotion some attention and accepting this is how you feel. By either leaning in, or using the labelling technique, you are showing respect to your body and mind by allowing the tension and stress of the emotion to release.

If the labelling technique doesn't feel enough, it could be that your emotion feels stuck, and you may recognise how your anger is a big charge of energy within your body. Stressful situations often get recorded in the central nervous system and will have passed into your blood chemistry through your hormones, peptides, and lipids. It will be part of the reason you hold yourself the way you do – it will be part of your joints, muscles, and fascia. Think about it – when anger hasn't been expressed, you may contain it within your jaw where it causes tension up into the back of your head and into your neck. In addition to this, you might make fists of your hands which spreads the tension up through the arms and into the shoulders. One way to release this is through movement which is designed to release the myofascia within the body (the myofascia is a network of tissue which is like a spider web of connectivity throughout the body). Movement which brings flexibility to the body, such as yoga,

Pilates, Qigong, and martial arts are all modalities which allow the body to move with the breath.

Mindful movement

In mindful movement, we are bringing present attention awareness to notice the way we move our body, and how it feels – this can be done with or without the breath being part of the focus. You can bring this awareness to any workout, or simply by walking. All you need to do is notice the way your body moves. Every time your mind wanders, you come back to your body and/or your breath.

So, you could bring this awareness when you are walking the dog or going to the bus stop. When you are next out for a run, you could be aware of your feet connecting with the ground. If you are swimming, you could notice how your feet move through the water. When on a bike, you could notice your ankles and how they help to provide the momentum of pushing down on the pedals.

Let's meditate: walking meditation

In a walking meditation, you notice how your body moves when you walk. You can be aware of the momentum of your feet whilst also being aware of the ground beneath you. You can notice your muscles in your legs, hips, torso, spine, arms, and head. You might notice your balance, your weight distribution as you move, your heart rate, your breathing, and even your temperature.

Start by being aware of the ground underneath your feet, connected to the earth.

Notice what is around you – take in your surroundings.

Begin to walk at a speed of your choice. Each time you raise your foot and return it to the ground, be aware of the movement throughout your body.

If your mind wanders, pause for a moment and feel the ground beneath your feet, before starting again.

If you want to, you can allow the flow of the breath to match with the flow of the movement. Or you can focus on a mantra. This could simply be counting one, two with each footstep, or focusing on the phrase 'I am here'.

If you find your thoughts are particularly distracting and your mind is drifting to stories and fantasies, you could bring in the naming technique to label the emotions generated by the stories.

In chapter five, I mention my dyspraxia diagnosis. Initially, I found the walking meditation to be tricky as it shone a spotlight on my balance issues. Continuing to work with this meditation has helped me to become more at home within my body as it is, and my balance has certainly improved. I enjoy incorporating this meditation with the naming technique when walking my dog. If I am distracted by the stories in my mind, I pause and label the emotions which have been generated by my thoughts, and then as I start to walk again, I listen to the sound of my feet on the ground before returning to awareness of the movement through my body. When my dog stops to explore her surroundings, I take this as an opportunity to stop with her and notice my surroundings. It's even fun to do short bursts of this when walking from room to room around the house.

The more you start bringing awareness to the what, when, and how of your anger, the more you can create the space to choose your response, improving your relationship with yourself. However, there are times when judgement can impact our experience, and so we will explore this in our next meditation foundation.

Chapter Ten:

Foundation: Non-judgement

Non-judgment is your friend

Throughout my life I had constantly measured all my experiences as either being a success or failure, right or wrong, good or bad. Unsurprisingly, I initially brought this type of measurement into my meditation practice too – I would judge myself for thinking as well as the types of thoughts I was having. I also judged my breath and my body too.

This all changed when I discovered one of the fundamental foundations of meditation is the practice of non-judgment.

But why do we feel the need to judge?

As human beings, we like to understand the actions and behaviours of ourselves and others. In psychology, this is referred to as 'attributions', which can be categorised as social or personal. From these, we make snap judgments about people and situations so we don't have to spend lots of time and energy processing what it going on.

This means we are hard-wired to judge as a form of survival, and therefore judging others is a natural instinct. According to Gabrielle Bernstein in her book *Judgment Detox*, 'We want to protect ourselves from that fear, so we project it outward in the form of judgment.'

Outwardly, we might be judging others, but when we bring the judgment inwards it can have a big impact on our meditation experience – when we judge, we create division and separation within ourselves.

Being hard on yourself

Do you expect more of yourself than you expect from others? After an evening out with friends, do you return home and analyse every aspect of the evening, looking for deeper meaning? Or worry about being misconstrued by your boss or friends? If you judge yourself in your everyday life, you will most certainly bring this into your meditation practice.

Judgment is a full stop

During your meditation practice, you will have the opportunity to view how you respond to things. Judgment will affect the flow of meditation: if you have been thinking and then you judge yourself for it, a flash of emotion such as frustration or irritation will rise and trigger an added-on story. With this interruption to your flow, it can mentally feel as if you have to climb over a mountain to get back to the concentrated focus – in fact, sometimes, the judgment can seem so encompassing it's like a big full stop within your practice.

When meditating you can remind yourself that you are the observer of what is happening – without judgment. So instead of judging the thought, the tone of thinking, or your aches and pains, you can be with 'what is' in a soft and gentle way.

Having compassion for yourself

The foundation in this chapter is about the practice of non-judgment. Bringing compassion to your practice will make this easier. According to the Dalai Lama, 'If you want others to be happy, practice compassion. If you want to be happy, practice compassion.' Being hard on yourself will only bring unease and discord and is not conducive to a flowing practice. Instead, bringing an element of friendliness, just like affection for an old friend, will bring a curious, gentle, and inquisitive mind, naturally placing you in the role of the observer. If you are not used to treating yourself with compassion, this may feel strange and self-indulgent at first, which is why practicing the loving-kindness meditation can be a tool to promote more positive feelings.

Metta meditation (loving-kindness)

The word *metta* comes from Pali – a language spoken in Northern India which is believed to be closely linked to Sanskrit. *Metta* is intended to produce a positive energy of kindness and when translated it is thought to mean love, kindness, compassion, benevolence, goodwill, and friendship. During the practice you offer phrases of compassion to yourself before wishing for others what you have wished for yourself. Usually this is towards friends and family, a stranger, and then the rest of the world. You can also include people who you are finding difficult.

Initially it can feel strange to offer compassion to yourself before offering to others. When I attended a Reiki One course many years ago, my reiki master asked me, 'Who is the most important person to you?' I started listing out all of my family members, whilst harbouring an anxious knot in my stomach as I worried I might miss one of them out. Eventually she stopped me and asked, 'Why have you not included yourself?'. Prior to this, it had never occurred to me that I could! But putting the needs of others first had meant I had ignored my own needs. Quite simply this had become exhausting.

To use the analogy of a bank account: if you are always paying out money without replenishing the funds, it will eventually become empty. It is the same with compassion: if you are always considering the needs of others without any consideration for yourself, eventually you will have nothing left to give.

The practice of any meditation is one way of giving back to yourself, but loving-kindness in particular is just like the water which replenishes a flower. You do not need to feel positive to do this practice, the idea is to just express intentions for both yourself and for others. The more you practice this, the easier it will become to let go of the harsh self-judgment, allowing you to improve your relationship with yourself.

Amazing impact on the brain and body

Would you like to increase your positive emotions whilst decreasing the negative ones? Would you like to curb your self-criticism? Would you like to improve your empathy as well as your social connections? Research has shown this meditation can help in all of these areas.

In David Hamilton's book *Why Kindness is Good for You* he explores how kindness and compassion alter the neural structures of our brains and can stimulate the nervous system to combat inflammation. He also looks at how love and kindness can be cardioprotective.

The first few times we do the full loving-kindness meditation, it can feel quite challenging especially if you are not used to extending any level of compassion towards yourself. Plus, the concept of saying the phrases for all sentient beings around the world might feel awkward or strange. For this reason, I have put together a few meditations as stepping stones towards the full loving-kindness practice.

Let's meditate: loving-kindness for a friend or family member

Sit or lie comfortably. Close your eyes, or place your gaze on a fixed spot in the room . . . .

Bring awareness to your breath, gently focusing on the in and out of your breath . . . .

As you continue to breathe in and out, bring a sense of ease with your breath to your heart space. You could always say inside your head, 'Breathing in I feel ease, breathing out I feel ease' . . . .

From this sense of ease in your heart space, bring a feeling of openness and warmth from your heart area. Just an intention is enough. Stay with this feeling for a moment, maybe feeling the warmth and openness radiating through your body . . . .

Bring to mind a friend or family member. Picture them or get a sense of their presence and feel the warmth from your heart radiating to theirs. And repeat to yourself the following phrases:

'May you be safe, may you be happy, may you be healthy, may you be at peace.'

If you find yourself focusing on the issues of your friend or family member, or your mind is wandering, it's OK. There is no need to judge. Just gently let go of those thoughts and instead offer the energy of well wishes from your heart to theirs . . . .

And continue to repeat 'May you be safe, may you be happy, may you be healthy, may you be at peace.'

Let's meditate: loving-kindness for a stranger

After a few days of practice, use the script above and bring the same level of compassion to a stranger. It could be someone you may see around, but you might not know their name. It could be a neighbour, someone you see when you walk the dog, someone at a bus stop or in a local shop.

Picture them now and get a sense of their presence. You may not know what is going on in their life, but you can know they need loving-kindness in their life just like you do. And feel the same level of warmth radiating from your heart to theirs as you repeat:

'May you be safe, may you be happy, may you be healthy, may you be at peace.'

Let's meditate: loving-kindness to all beings everywhere

After a few days of practice, use the scripts above and bring the same level of compassion to everyone, everywhere.

Picture, or sense, all friends, family members, neighbours, the community. Extend this to all pets and animals, all species. Feel the warmth radiating from your heart to all beings everywhere. And repeat:

'May we all be safe, may we all be happy, may we all be healthy, may we all be at peace.'

Let's meditate: loving-kindness the full practice, starting with yourself

Listen to this audio meditation at sarahpresley.co.uk/making-friends-with-yourself/meditations

Sitting or lying comfortably, close your eyes or place your gaze on a non-moving spot.

Bring awareness to your breath, gently focusing on the in and out of your breath . . . .

As you continue to breathe in and out, bring a sense of ease with your breath to your heart space. You could always say inside your head, 'Breathing in I feel ease, breathing out I feel ease' . . . .

You may start to feel an openness and warmth from your heart area, however, just an intention is enough . . . .

From your heart space, begin to repeat these open phrases to yourself:

'May I be safe, may I be happy, may I be healthy, may I be at peace. May I be safe, may I be happy, may I be healthy, may I be at peace' . . . .

If your mind is creating reasons not to feel loving-kindness towards yourself right now, it's OK. There is no need to judge. You can always surrender your negative thoughts and feelings on the out breath, and then come back to focusing on repetition of the phrases rather than the meaning.

And continue to repeat 'may I be safe, may I be happy, may I be healthy, may I be at peace'. . . .

Now return to your heart space and bring to mind someone in your life who is in need of loving-kindness right now. It could be a friend or family member. Picture them or get a sense of their presence and feel the warmth from your heart radiating to theirs. You can wish for them, what you have wished for yourself. And repeat:

'May you be safe, may you be happy, may you be healthy, may you be at peace. May you be safe, may you be happy, may you be healthy, may you be at peace'. . . .

If you find yourself focusing on the issues of your friend or family member, or your mind is wandering, it's OK. There is no need to judge. Just gently let go of your thoughts and instead offer the energy of well wishes from your heart to theirs. And repeat, 'May you be safe, may you be happy, may you be healthy, may you be at peace'. . . .

Now return to your heart space and this time bring to mind a stranger. Someone you may see around, but you might not know their name. It could be a neighbour, someone you see when you walk the dog, someone at a bus stop or in a local shop. Picture them now or get a sense of their presence. You may not know what is going on in their life, but you can know they need loving-kindness in their life just like you do. And feel the same level of warmth radiating from your heart to theirs as you repeat, 'May you be safe, may you be happy, may you be healthy, may you be at peace.

May you be safe, may you be happy, may you be healthy, may you be at peace'. . . .

Now returning once again to the warmth and ease of loving-kindness at your heart, extend your well-wishes to everyone everywhere. To all friends, family members, neighbours, the community. To all pets and animals, to all species. Feel the warmth radiating from your heart to all beings everywhere. And repeat:

'May we all be safe, may we all be happy, may we all be healthy, may we all be at peace. May we all be safe, may we all be happy, may we all be healthy, may we all be at peace'. . . .

Now feel a sense of the loving-kindness radiating back to you. Just for a moment allow yourself to receive the well wishes from someone somewhere who is saying these phrases to you. Allow your heart to open and receive.

Now gently come back to feeling your feet on the ground, your breath at your nose. And when you feel ready, gently, open your eyes.

It's not always easy, but it's a start

The first time I attempted this meditation, I found it challenging. It's not surprising as I had always been so hard on myself, but I also knew I needed to make a change as I was only making myself feel unhappy. I knew if I wanted to treat myself in a better way it would be worth persevering.

If you found it challenging too, remember the first time is the starting point to something new.

When you learnt to walk, you will have fallen over a number of times before you learnt to find balance. It is the same with this meditation. The more I practiced, the more I began to find the flow and more importantly I discovered this was having an affect outside the practice too – whilst berating myself one day for a perceived wrongdoing, I found myself easily allowing the negative thought to drift away and making room for a much more positive one. And it felt great!

I have also seen this meditation benefit those around me. Some years ago, a friend who worked as a cleaner was going through a rough time. I explained the concept of loving-kindness to her and suggested she repeated the phrases to herself whilst cleaning at work. When I saw her a couple of weeks later, she looked amazing! Her difficult life situation hadn't improved, but the way she was treating herself had.

When my eldest son was ten years old, he started struggling with his feelings, and in his unhappy state he would brood and his bottom lip would protrude. Desperate to help him, I encouraged him to talk about how he was feeling, and despite my best attempts, it just didn't seem to help. Eventually I taught him loving-kindness and we worked every day on focusing on the wishes of loving-kindness towards himself. Two weeks later he was so much more content and happier with life. When he was fifteen, I was talking to him about his meditation experience and asked him which meditation had felt transformative for him, and if he had a favourite. On both counts he said it was 'the meditation where you say nice things to yourself.' It was so great to hear he had recognised the difference it had made.

You can use any phrases which feel right for you and your situation, such as 'may I feel safe', or 'may I be free of suffering', or 'may I be well'. You could even say 'may I feel strong', or 'may I feel confident', or 'may I feel loved'. Use the phrases which feel applicable to your own life so you can connect with them on a more meaningful basis.

The more I practice this meditation and see the positive effects it brings, the more I can see how much we can all benefit from more compassion towards ourselves. But what about when the inner critic pops up and interferes with the flow of our present moment? In the next chapter we will look at why we have an inner critic and how we can turn to mindfulness to help us.

Chapter Eleven:

Making Friends With Your Inner Critic

'You have nothing of interest to say. Everyone is going to think you are stupid'. I could hear these words as I was about to walk on stage to sing with my band, and the voice was curt and full of scorn.

Just moments before I had been looking forward to the gig, but now my feet were not sure if they wanted to move and my heart felt like it had plunged into my stomach. I tried to ignore the voice, and although my feet felt like they were encased in concrete, I began to walk slowly towards the stage again. After a few difficult steps, I could hear the voice again and it was louder this time. 'You are about to make a fool out of yourself!', it shouted. I wanted to turn around and tell it to stop – but I couldn't. The voice was in me.

It was the voice of my inner critic.

Singing has always given me an immense amount of joy – I have never considered myself to be the best singer in the world, but I have always felt the movement of music and song lyrics inside of me and I enjoy being part of the conduit of energy in conveying their meaning. Part of the package of being a singer has involved 'entertaining' the audience between songs and I had grown up admiring singers who engaged with their audience throughout their shows. However, when I needed to connect with my audience in between songs, my inner critic would communicate my deepest fear of not being interesting enough.

On the outside, no one would have guessed this about me as I appear to be confident and outgoing. So, out of fear of appearing weak or silly, I never told anyone about my inner doubts. I hoped the feeling would disappear, but it didn't. Over time my inner voice confirmed that I was not interesting, fun, or smart enough for the audiences we played to. At the end of each song I would be willing myself to say something meaningful, but my mind would go blank and instead I would say something inane, such as 'Hands up if you like the colour purple!' In desperation, prior to the gigs I would attempt to write scripts for myself that were witty and entertaining, but my inner critic would speak up and doubt would drop back in. I would become paralysed with fear, and this served to prove my inner critic right.

Most of us have experienced a self-critical and self-doubting inner dialogue at some time in our lives. As well as being called the inner critic, it is also referred to as the self-saboteur, or as the imposter syndrome. It can rise out of nowhere and speak of your most clandestine anxieties and frustrations. Its voice can be judgemental, disapproving, and critical. Your inner critic can be a perfectionist that wants you to be the best in your job and will say, 'this work is not good enough, other people are much better at this than you'. It can undermine your confidence and tell you 'you're not fun' when you are about to meet up with friends. It might say 'you are unlovable' so you end up adapting your beliefs and actions within your relationships. It can tell you, 'you are wrong', 'you are ugly' or 'you are rubbish' in a voice which is mean, degrading, unkind and unpleasant. It can stop you from speaking up, trying new things, and living a happy life.

Why it speaks to you

We all have an inner voice which is constantly reviewing the here and now, as well as the past and the future, and it comes from the natural instinct we all have for safety. At times, the inner voice may be positive, praising you for a job well-done, being understanding or even encouraging. At other times it can be mean and critical. According to Dr. Kristen Neff, author of *The Mindful Self Compassion Workbook*, 'If we look closely – our inner critic cares'.

Psychologists believe our inner critic is formed from our core beliefs which come from our childhood, where we aim to make sense of our experiences. As a child, if you were often criticised for speaking out, you may develop an inner critic voice which prevents you from doing this as an adult. Or if you were bullied at school, your inner critic may aim to adjust your behaviour to prevent the same from happening in work situations.

None of us want to experience embarrassment, shame, or a feeling of failure, and so your inner critic will speak to you in a harsh voice if it perceives you to be entering into something which may result in vulnerability. It is attempting to awaken you. However, this part of the psyche doesn't understand that risk is an important factor in growth. It doesn't know that instead of protection, it is bringing great suffering.

Why compassion works

My first step to making friends with my inner critic came from my mindfulness practice, whereby I was able to understand how I no longer needed to be attached, or to act, on every thought I had. The act of mindfulness allows me to view my thoughts without judging them, so I was able to observe my negative dialogue and the impact it had on my body, emotions and thoughts. Within this observation I was able to create a space where I could take steps to understand my relationship with my inner critic, and whilst in this place, I discovered it was just trying to protect me.

If a friend or family member vocalised a harsh or highly critical thought about themselves, you would recognise they were in a state of suffering. In this instance you would be happy to open your heart to compassion for them, perhaps giving them a hug or words of encouragement. What would happen if you extended this same principle to yourself? When you are being harsh or highly critical of yourself, you could recognise that this places you in a state of suffering and you can open up your heart to compassion for yourself. Christopher Germer, author of *The Mindful Path to Self-Compassion*, says 'Compassion is simply giving the same kindness to ourselves that we would give to others'.

Opening yourself to self-compassion could be quite simply repeating an open phrase, such as one of the ones we practiced in the *metta* meditation in the previous chapter. You could choose a phrase which has meaning to you, like 'may I be safe' or 'may I feel love', or a visualisation such as imagining yourself surrounded by a love heart, enveloped in a great big bear hug or filled up with a healing white light. Just holding yourself with self-compassion means the negative feeling, brought on by the inner critic, can gradually dissolve – you will be soothing your stressed state with kindness. With each passing moment, you can then gently allow yourself to disconnect from the negative voice. The more you practice this, the more you can recognise that your inner critic voice acts as a reminder to offer yourself self-compassion.

When I am walking onto stage now, I can recognise the moment of doubt as just that – a moment. I am able to view it as an opportunity for nurture and transformation, and a reason to envelop myself with compassion. I can embrace myself as perfectly imperfect, and know it is OK not to have everything figured out, and use every experience on stage to learn and grow. I can whisper back to my inner critic 'Thanks for looking out for me – but it's OK, I've got it from here'.

Let's be mindful: STOP – a mindfulness and self-compassion technique

S for STOP: When you have a harsh and unkind thought, take a moment to pause and identify it as the inner critic.

T for TUNE IN: Allow yourself to feel space between yourself and the thought to bring awareness without changing anything. Is the thought bringing tension to your body? What about your emotions? Your thoughts? Just allow it all to be there without attempting to ignore or push it away.

O for OBSERVE: Notice the thought is coming from a place of vulnerability and therefore creating a feeling of suffering. As you observe this, be aware of any changes this brings to your body, emotions, or thoughts.

P for PRACTICE: Bring in a feeling of self-compassion. In this moment, think about how you would hold a friend who was having a hard time with harsh thoughts – would you offer up a hug or reassuring words? Now bring this same sense of compassion to yourself. Allow your heart and mind to soften.

There is an old proverb which says 'practice makes perfect'. This saying is not to say we, as individuals, become perfect – but instead the more you practice, the easier something becomes. To make friends with the inner critic is to understand our relationship with it. To practice self-compassion at difficult times means we are able to view ourselves with more of a friendliness and ease, and take steps to understand why we feel the way we do.

The more we practice mindfulness, the more we are able to accept each moment 'as is'. In the next chapter, we will look at why this is an important foundation within our meditation practice.

Chapter Twelve:

Meditation Foundation: Acceptance

Every moment is your friend

Throughout this book we have been discovering how meditation is training your attention to be in the present moment. As you make your way through the meditations and start to incorporate them into your week, you may discover you are already being much more present in your everyday life. The training of your attention will lead you to be more mindful. It may be a fleeting moment where you notice the colours of the leaves on a tree, or it might be noticing the aroma of your cup of coffee. You may even find you are beginning to find space when you observe your thoughts, rather than feeling tangled inside of them.

In meditation we are not looking for every moment to be perfect, but instead showing up to be present with *what is,* and for the most part, this feels OK. But what happens when the moment feels stuck or uncomfortable?

It doesn't always flow the way you want it to

Sometimes we can't always get into the flow and yet we might not be able to understand why: you know the mind will wander, and you know you need to bring it back, but everything just feels so much harder. You might be using the naming technique from chapter eight, yet your mind keeps yo-yoing back to thoughts and feelings. When this happens frustration can loom, and the act of compassion may seem out of reach, so the meditation feels uncomfortable and hard to stick with.

Attempting to understand why the moment isn't feeling right adds to the struggle: asking yourself *why* will mean a cycle of thought begins, which may not give you the answer you are looking for and instead compounds the issue by adding strong emotions and tension to the body. So forming an attachment to the thoughts here is certainly not going to help.

Instead, understanding how you are resisting the experience is going to be key: the stuck feeling is *the present moment*, but maybe you are feeling it should be something different. This is where bringing a mindfulness curiosity can help you accept the situation.

Letting go of the goals

To feel in the flow, we have to be accepting of where we are, moment to moment. Yet this is not always easy: maybe we like the moment we were in before when there were feelings of peace or joy or happiness, so we are fearful of how we might feel when we let these feelings go. We may have a preconceived idea of how we *should* feel, for instance 'I should be relaxed', or 'I should be able to focus by now.'

We are used to setting goals in life, so it is easy to bring them to the meditation cushion – but goals are going to get in the way of the experience and just create more pressure. As we are finding out, there are some amazing health and well-being benefits to a meditation practice, but these are the by-products of the experience and should not be intended as the goal when you sit down to meditate.

Acceptance

Having an acceptance of where you are in the current moment will help to remove the stress and you can achieve this by witnessing the resistance and allowing it to be there within your meditation experience.

When we take the step to view the situation with curiosity, we are reminded we are the observer rather than the participator. It's just like watching a movie – most of the time you know you are watching a movie with actors and sets (observing), but there are other times when you are inside the plot, shouting at the TV set, 'don't walk down the stairs in the dark – switch the lights on so you can see the man hiding in the shadows!' (the participator). Once the action has unfolded, we remind ourselves it's only a movie (back to being the observer). It's the same with our meditation practice. The resistance might make us the participator ('why isn't the meditation flowing' or 'why can't I meditate today'), but simply stepping into acceptance can bring us back to being the observer ('how interesting I am feeling resistance right now'). We can then step back to the naming technique and label resistance – we might have to do this a few times, but after a while the resistance can lift, and the mediation can flow once again.

Having acceptance doesn't mean you have to like the moment you are in, nor is it a passive place to be. Acceptance means you no longer fight what is real and happening right now. When you accept, you realise the resistance you were holding before was only creating suffering for yourself.

Recognising my resistance to the uncomfortable moments in meditation also allowed me to be more aware of when I was resisting in everyday life, too. When attending a Reiki One course many years ago, one of the course subjects was looking at how we can have gratitude for all the little moments in our life. I found myself struggling with this concept – I was ill and life felt difficult, so I couldn't see what there was to be feel grateful about. I felt uncomfortable with the discussion and my body tensed up. My reiki master noticed this and asked me if I was always focusing on the negatives in my life. 'Yes', I responded. 'Hmmm', she replied, 'How is that working for you?' Straight away, I realised I was the participator in my own misery, and so I observed my discomfort and then gently allowed myself to let it go. I realised if I continued to focus on what was wrong with my life, I would continue to live a life feeling ill and unhappy. In accepting the moment of resistance, it became a powerful trigger for change.

Quite often we will find ourselves in a negative bias, focusing on everything that is wrong. This is a natural place to be, as our brains are designed to look for threats and danger in order to keep us safe. But with all of the psychological threats around us, we will always be bracing ourselves for *what's next.* So what happens when we choose to also focus on what is right in our world? It doesn't mean we have to be dismissive of the wrongs, but instead we can recognise how we can have an appreciation of all things in life and allow our minds to find a better balance. For instance, our negative bias may look at a grey sky and worry how the rain might ruin the day. But a more balanced mind might still notice the grey sky but may also acknowledge the amazing shades of grey, and appreciate how the rain will help the plants and trees to thrive and grow. Or a negative mind might dwell on a broken night's sleep and be concerned about how that will affect us during the following day. Yet a balanced mind will still acknowledge the broken sleep but feel grateful for the bed which supported the body, the duvet which kept us warm, and know that there will be an opportunity to rest or catch up on sleep another time.

The gratitude meditation in particular can help us to be reflective in this area and can bring incredible changes to our bodies and minds.

Studies have shown that gratitude can bring benefits to health and wellbeing and that by having a regular practice of focusing on the blessings in our world, it can boost our happiness as well as help us with perceived stress. It has also been shown to benefit our sleep.

Gratitude meditation

This type of meditation is a reflection meditation where you practice acknowledging the things in your life you are grateful for. It might be the big things like your home, car, or job, as well as the simple things such as a beautiful sunset, or a cup of tea and a chat with a friend. Instead of focusing on what is wrong with your body, you could pick one aspect of it which you are grateful for. Or acknowledge all the wonderful inventions which make your life smoother. or bring an awareness of the fact that difficulties in life present an opportunity for learning and growth.

At first this type of meditation may feel challenging as you may be used to focusing on what is wrong. But see if you can open yourself up to acknowledging at least one thing in your life which you can feel grateful for today. And remember, today is a starting point to something new.

Let's meditate: gratitude

Listen to this audio meditation at sarahpresley.co.uk/making-friends-with-yourself/meditations

Close your eyes, or place them on a fixed spot in the room . . . . Connect with your breath coming in and out of your body . . . Let your attention rest gently on your breath and feel each movement of it . . . . As you breathe out, feel yourself letting go of tension. Relax your face. Your shoulders. Your chest and abdomen. Your arms and hands. And your legs and feet . . . .

Bring your attention to your heart space, feeling a sense of ease here with each breath. Allow yourself to relax into the feeling . . . .

Now imagine there is a central line of gratitude which comes from the earth through the centre of your body. Feel it connect through your heart space. Don't worry if you don't feel it straight away. When you feel ready, you can always surrender yourself to the experience, and let go of any judgement or reasons not to feel grateful today . . . .

Bring a sense of gratitude to your breath, your friend, that is always there for you. The simple art of breathing which your body does naturally. In meditation it introduces a relaxation response to your body so that all the systems of your body can feel calmer . . . . Just for today, just for this moment you can feel grateful for your breath . . . .

Now bring the sense of gratitude to your body. We often focus on what is wrong with our bodies, but what happens if you focus on what is right? Even if it is just one thing. Our bodies are the vehicle in which we are able to sense and experience life, so let's explore this sensory system. Firstly, focus on what you are able to see: a beautiful smile, the sky, the sea and all of nature in its wonderful glory, the most incredible array of colours . . . . Now, what you are able to hear: the sound of laughter, music, rustling of wind in the trees, the vibrational sound of the comings and goings of everyday life . . . . Next, what you are able to smell: flowers, the sea, the aroma of a cup of coffee, the scent of someone you love . . . .Now, what you are able to taste: your toothpaste, your favourite food, even the air . . . . And finally what you can feel through your hands and feet and all of your body: the breeze running through your hair, a hug, a kiss, holding someone's hand . . . . Just for today, just for this moment you can feel grateful for your body . . . .

Now bring a sense of gratitude to your life. There are always going to be twists and turns and ups and downs, but every experience offers us the ability to learn and grow. We often focus on what is wrong with our lives, but what happens when you focus on what is right? Scan through your day and you may notice the bed which supported you throughout the night, your warm shower or bath, your breakfast or lunch which nourished and fueled your body. And as you scan your day, if you find your focus falls on the negative aspects, let them go. Just for today, just for this moment, you can feel grateful for your life . . . .

Now bring the sense of gratitude to the people in your life. Your life is enriched with a variety of people. Think of those who have supported you at different times of your life. The people you have shared fun times and laughter with. Then those who have made your life run smoother. And what about the people you have loved? Just for today, just for this moment, you can feel grateful for all the wonderful people in your life . . . .

Next bring a sense of gratitude to all the things in your life which make life easier. There is your home, your car, your shower, your phone, your computer. You may only notice these things when they go wrong. But what about all the times when they work well and contribute to an easier flow of life? Just for today, just for this moment, you can feel grateful for all the wonderful things in your life . . . .

Now come back to the sense of ease in your heart space. And just for today, just for this moment, acknowledge yourself and the things you do. For the times you reached out and checked on friends and family. The times when you have created beautiful meals, driven people to appointments, or picked up some shopping for someone in need. Then there are the gifts you have given on special occasions. Acknowledge the thought and care you have given to others and bring a sense of gratefulness for all the things you do . . . .

Now come back to your body and connect once again to the central line of gratitude which runs from the earth and through your body. Connect once again to the ease at your heart space. And when you are ready, gently open your eyes.

Hopefully there was at least one thing you could feel grateful for today, and remember, just one aspect is a step in the right direction to a calmer and more balanced mindset.

Some people acknowledge three moments of gratefulness before going to bed and find they drift off to sleep feeling much more positive. When my children were nine and five, I decided to bring the concept to my family and set up a jar labelled 'Things which make me feel happy' in our kitchen. I explained how we could all acknowledge the good things about one another and write them down on a piece of paper and read them out at the end of the year. They all did a lot of eye rolling at the suggestion, so I decided that even if they didn't take part, I would still go ahead and write down the things I had noticed about them throughout the year. When we opened the jar, it was full – everyone had taken part, and we had a great time reminding ourselves of all the positive experiences we had with one another.

Acceptance is key to the flow of life, but what happens if we feel the pain of rejection? In this next chapter we can understand why it feels painful and how we can turn to our meditation experience.

Chapter Thirteen:

Making Friends With Rejection and Pain

When going through a tough time a number of years ago, I reached out to a friend. I was seeking compassion and understanding but instead she expressed anger and frustration, and in no uncertain terms told me to 'get on with it'. Opening up at such a vulnerable time made her reaction hurtful and the rejection felt like a stab in my heart.

Rejection has featured throughout my life in various degrees, and my earliest memory was when I was six years old. One day I was playing together with two friends, the next day they wanted to play without me. I can still recall the confusion and hurt I felt at the time. The next day we were back to normal again, but rejection would reappear again – there were the times I wasn't selected for team sports, or a part in a school play, asked out by a boy I liked, or invited to a party. Then later in my work life, there were the times I wasn't selected for promotion, or my insights and ideas weren't listened to. The more I experienced rejection, the more devastating and cumulative the effect, impacting not only my self-esteem but also my sense of trust and belonging.

When relaying the conversation about my friend with another friend, she offered me a different perspective: 'You don't know what is going on in her life right now', she said. And yes, she was right, I didn't know if she was going through a tough time herself, or if she lacked the confidence to be able to help a friend in need, or if she really didn't care. Any story I was creating was based on fiction with no tangible facts, and was a complete waste of energy. In other words, it was my friend's business as to why she rejected me, and it was *my* business as to how I would deal with her rejection.

We can feel rejection on so many different levels: from the smaller levels of being 'unfriended' on social media, to someone not replying to your text, to the bigger levels, where your love for someone else is not reciprocated or you don't get the job you have set all of your hopes on. For some it can be easy to brush off rejection, but for others it can feel harder. It can often produce an inner narrative response where you play out stories within your mind to try to make sense of what has happened. You may begin to ruminate over what has gone wrong, finding yourself replaying conversations over and over again, pulling them apart from every angle and analysing every single inch. You may even begin to feel you have deserved the rejection and your inner critic begins to have a field day, highlighting all of your negative aspects.

Why does rejection hurt?

The way our brain processes our emotions is completely different to how our brain processes physical pain, except when it comes to the hurt we feel from rejection. Neuroscientists have discovered the area which becomes activated when we are in pain is the same area which becomes activated when we are rejected. In other words, rejection literally is painful.

Psychologists believe we are hard-wired to feel rejection in such a painful way from an evolutionary point of view. Back when we lived in tribes, surviving alone would have been difficult, so being rejected could ultimately mean death. Having an inbuilt system that warns us rejection could be painful means we would have adjusted our behaviour to stay within the tribe.

The reason we all deal with rejection differently is because when we feel physical or social pain, the brain will naturally release Mu opioids which act as painkillers. For some, the level of opioids will be higher than others.

Taking care of your business

In chapter twelve, we looked at how we can experience resistance when meditation isn't flowing the way we hoped it would. It is the same in our everyday lives too – sometimes life does not flow in a way we can accept, and therefore we reject the way it is. Without acceptance, however, our feelings will be bunched up inside, and our thoughts will be in an ever-decreasing circle of despair.

But accepting rejection doesn't mean we condone the behaviour of another. Instead, we understand that without acceptance we will continue to have an inner conflict which results in promoting more fear and pain.

There is a popular legend known as 'The Two Wolves', which is often attributed to the Cherokee people, in which a grandfather uses the metaphor of two wolves fighting within to explain inner conflict.

'My son' he said to the boy. 'The battle is between two wolves inside us all. One is evil. It is anger, envy, jealousy, sorrow, regret, greed, arrogance, self-pity, guilt, resentment, inferiority, lies, false pride, superiority, and ego.'

He continued, 'The other is good. It is joy, peace, love, hope, serenity, humility, kindness, benevolence, empathy, generosity, truth, compassion, and faith.'

The grandson thought about it for a minute and then asked his grandfather, 'Which wolf will win?'

The old Cherokee simply replied, 'The one you feed.'

When experiencing rejection we have the two wolves fighting inside of us, the one which wants to hold onto the hurt and perhaps seek revenge, and the other which wants to find peace and an inner resolution. When we recognise this, we realise we have the choice of which one we want to feed.

Connecting with peace

If we learn to have acceptance, even when there is chaos around us, we can start to listen, to a greater degree to the silence within, residing in the space between our breath and our thoughts and feelings. When we access this space, we can start to connect much more to a sense of peace inside, where we can feel grounded, yet also connected.

The expression 'being grounded' has been around for years and relates to a feeling of being mentally and physically at ease. When grounded, it is easier to feel calm and present as you are in your body, feeling centred and balanced whilst also feeling connected to the earth. When ungrounded, you can feel anxious, restless, overwhelmed, stressed, and distracted.

If we choose to find peace, we can create a mindful moment to realise how the situation is creating tension in our mind and body and turn to the meditation foundations we have learnt in this book.

BE AWARE OF YOUR BREATH: take some conscious breaths. This will allow the relaxation response to kick in and remind your body you are now in a safe place. The breath will be the anchor to the present moment, so you can begin to be the observer of yourself in the here and now.

BE AWARE OF YOUR BODY: as you continue with the breath, be aware of your body too. Are there areas which are tense? Do you want to hold onto the tension, or will you allow the breath to dissolve it?

BE AWARE OF DISTRACTIONS: is your mind going back to stories or playing over the event? Do you want to stay with this, or do you want to come back to the soothing breath? What about your emotions? Do you want to lean into them and continue to observe them, or do you want to allow them to leave on your out breath?

BE AWARE OF JUDGEMENT: if you are judging yourself harshly, do you want to hold onto your beliefs, or do you want to bring compassion for yourself in this moment? In what way can you bring compassion to yourself right now? You could always repeat some of the loving-kindness phrases to yourself or imagine yourself surrounded by love.

ACCEPT: allow yourself to accept the moment as it is, and then continue to repeat the steps above – staying with your breath, being aware of your body, distractions, and judgement, before returning to acceptance of 'what is'.

Just like a mountain, we can become rooted in the earth as we start to feel strong and steady. We can feel an uplift from inside, as if our spine is the centre of the mountain, feeling more stability within us. With our head and neck like the lofty peak of the mountain, we can feel connected with what is going on. Through the ever-changing weather of our lives, thoughts and feelings, we can remain as the mountain: just sitting, observing, and connecting to moments of peace between our breath and distractions.

Let's meditate: peace

Listen to this audio meditation at sarahpresley.co.uk/making-friends-with-yourself/meditations

Close your eyes or place your eyes on a non-moving spot. Be aware of your feet on the ground, connected to the earth, and feel an uplift inside . . . .

Notice sounds around you, coming and going . . . . The sounds will be the backdrop to your meditation experience, so let them be there . . . .

Now, gently let go of sounds and be aware of your breath, coming in and out of your body. Allow it to find it's natural rhythm . . . . Your thoughts will begin to come and go too, but when you feel distracted, gently come back to noticing your breath, coming in, and then going back out . . . .

Imagine, pretend, or get a sense, that peace is coming into your body. If you like, you can imagine it travelling in with your breath . . . . Or you could imagine peace as a colour, or even as a feeling . . . . Or you could repeat the word 'peace' inside your head . . . . Go with whatever feels good for you right now . . . .

As your breath is coming in and out, imagine peace is travelling down your body and reaching your feet and toes . . . .

Now imagine it filling up your legs and pelvis . . . your torso . . . your arms, hands, fingers, and thumbs . . . . Feel it coming up into your neck and your head . . . . so you are completely filled up with peace . . . .

As peace flows in, imagine that peace flows out too. See it surrounding you and touching every part of your skin . . . . So you are filled up and surrounded by peace . . . .

As peace flows in, and as peace flows out, imagine it is spreading out into the room that you are in . . . . See it touching every wall, the ceiling, the floor, window, and door . . . . As you continue to be filled up and surrounded by peace . . . .

As peace flows in, and as peace flows out, imagine it seeping under the doorway, moving through every room of the building you are in . . . . As you continue to be filled up and surrounded by peace . . . .

As peace flows in, and as peace flows out, imagine it spreading out across the city outside, touching every road and building . . . . As you continue to be filled up and surrounded by peace . . . .

As peace flows in, and as peace flows out, imagine it going across fields . . . . through woods . . . . across hills . . . . forests . . . and mountains . . .

. As you continue to be filled up and surrounded by peace . . . .

As peace flows in, and as peace flows out, imagine it going across streams and rivers . . . . across lakes . . . and oceans . . . As you continue to be filled up and surrounded by peace . . . .

As peace flows in, and as peace flows out, imagine it going across our beautiful planet, Mother Earth . . . . see it going to all the people . . . . all animals . . . . to all species . . . . As you continue to be filled up and surrounded by peace . . . .

As peace flows in, and as peace flows out, imagine it spreading up to the Universe . . . going to the sun and the moon . . . the stars, and all the planets in the sky . . . . As you continue to be filled up, and surrounded, by peace . . . .

As peace flows in, and as peace flows out, imagine the Universe sending peace back to you . . . . feel it connect with your heart, as it moves in through your body . . . . moving down through your torso, to your feet and your toes . . . . down your arms . . . . and into your head and neck . . . . So you can take this peaceful feeling with you for the rest of your day . . . .

Now, be aware of your feet on the ground, connected to the earth and your head amongst the stars. You are grounded yet connected . . . . And then when you are ready, gently open your eyes.

The effects of meditation are cumulative, so the more you do, the more you will benefit from all the wonderful health and well-being benefits. In the final chapter, let's look at how we can bring these incredible life-changing skills into our everyday life.

Chapter Fourteen:

Meditation for Life

When COVID hit in March 2020, I don't think anything could have prepared us for the shockwaves around the world. At this point, I had been teaching meditation for several years, as well as maintaining my own daily practice, and I was already working on the concept of this book. A few months prior, I had joined a writing group to improve my writing skills and I had also been freelancing for a UK mindfulness magazine as their meditation 'expert'. Life felt good – I had been enjoying great health for numerous years, and I loved my work and my family life.

When we entered lockdown, I initially felt OK and that I had all the tools I needed for dealing with the changes in life. But things began to change – the workload for both my husband and I increased, yet we still needed to support our sons with their home learning and well-being. My stepdad became hospitalised and later passed away, so we were supporting my mum whilst processing the grief from our loss too. Then, when we were out for a walk one day, a pipe burst, and half of our house suffered water damage.

Everything felt like it was snowballing around me and, although I was short on time, I decided to increase my meditation practice. I started calling it 'my daily devotion' and I would awake a little earlier every morning and commit to the foundations of meditation. Although life was difficult, I had the tools to help me navigate through the tough situations with equilibrium – to maintain a friendship with myself.

This book has been written for you as a starting point to something new. Within it we have taken a journey to discover the best foundations for a meditation practice whilst also understanding why we feel the way we do. We have learnt how meditation is training our attention to be present, so we can be much more aware of what is happening in the present moment rather than ruminating over the past or feeling anxious about the future.

We have discovered how the breath is the first foundation – as well as being a tool for focused awareness, it can be the beginning and end of all meditations and can be used in bite-sized chunks throughout the day. Through the breath, we can remind our body that we are safe and reconnect with calm and relaxation.

We also no longer need to ignore or push away the tension in our bodies, and instead can allow the breath to bring relief, so that we can feel more at home within our body by being witness to the sensations.

When thoughts and sounds distract us, we no longer need to get caught up within the stories they create and instead we can be the observer, allowing ourselves to gently label the distractions. We can also bring compassion to ourselves when we recognise that we have stepped into judgment, and learn to accept every moment, regardless of what it is.

We have also discovered how the body will naturally respond to stress by inducing feelings of anxiety, worry, anger and we might also experience the inner critic and the pain of rejection. In understanding why we feel the way we do, we learn how to hold ourselves with compassion and care and turn to our meditation practice to help us ride out the intensity of these feelings.

We can turn to a wide range of meditations – as well as the breath, the body scan and mindful labelling, there is also the mantra, the walking meditation, loving-kindness, gratitude, visualisation, and the STOP technique. We can also know that sometimes it can feel easy to meditate, and sometimes it can be hard, but even in the hard times we can learn a lot about ourselves as well as the practice itself.

If you continue to commit to the practice, you will be investing in your health and well-being. You will be promoting positive techniques which you can bring into every aspect of your day. You will feel more control with your emotions, and less reactive when things are not running smoothly, or life is changing. You will begin to see the wide variety of choices in front of you – the choice to stay within the chaos of your thoughts, or the opportunity to lean into the feelings or let them go. This will result in feeling more resilient in the face of adversity. You will have better concentration and will feel much more focused, as well as more connected to yourself, others, and nature. You will see that every passing moment offers you the opportunity to be the witness of the good, the bad, and everything in between, and what a joy it is to be in the vehicle of your body and to have these experiences.

But above all else, you will have the tools to take you from overwhelm to the peace which resides within you and make friends with who you are.

So now is the time to commit to the practice and create your own daily devotion.

Thank you for reading this book and taking a step towards a new beginning. You can continue to use the meditation recordings through the links. You can also find out more about meditation via my website: www.sarahpresley.co.uk. If you would like to take steps to support others with their meditation practice, join us on our British School of Meditation externally accredited meditation teachers' course: www.teaching-meditation.co.uk.

Acknowledgments

I started writing this book six years ago, but the ideas have formulated over a twenty year period - every time I have learnt something new, I have had an overwhelming desire to share it with others.

My husband, Andy, has been my constant sounding board, as well as championing me every step of the way. Thanks doesn't come close to acknowledging his support and belief in me.

My two sons, Eden and Cal, are the inspiration behind my desire to be the best I can be. My heart bursts with pride as I witness the wise, kind and thoughtful men they are becoming.

I have an amazing family – what an incredible journey we have been on together. If I had to do it all over again, I would choose every single one of you to be by my side.

The same goes for my friends – Jenny S, Emma, Amy, Sue, Helen, Sherry, Kate, Jenny P, Becca, Karen, Cath, and Nic.

When I was exploring the best way to restore my health and well-being, Sian Thomas and Katherine Brooks gave unwavering support with their complementary therapy treatments – thank you for helping me to dig out from the tunnel I had found myself in. More recently, I have turned to

Lauren Manning, and have found her wise words to always come at the right time.

Nadia, I am grateful for all the knowledge you imparted when I was training to be a reiki master. I have the fondest memories of the time I spent with you, Marion, Jane, Fay, and Debbie.

Mary Pearson and Helen Galpin, it has been an honour to be one of your British School of Meditation trainers. Your belief in me as a teacher has always been unwavering.

I'm excited about the next chapter as co-owner of this wonderful organisation alongside Catherine Banks and Catherine Thomlinson, and already my life has been enriched by sharing this incredible journey with you both.

When I had the skeleton of this book, my path crossed with Hannah Gold who invited me into her beautiful sanctuary, and helped me with the steps to find my authors voice. It has been a joy to witness you becoming a successful author and inspire a young generation with your passion for animals and climate concerns.

Rosalie Love, thank you for your amazing editing eye. And thanks, too, to Emma Coxon for being the first person to read the manuscript – your enthusiasm gave me the encouragement I needed to take the next step. Becca Lightfoot, I am also grateful you wielded your pencil and proofread at short notice.

Working with Louise Kelly on the book design has been a beautiful process, and both you and

Wayne Inker have been a wonderful team in developing my website too.

My friend, Matt, thank you for demystifying the self-publishing process – your amazing calm presence and knowledge helped get me to get this book over the finish line.

To all of those who have stepped through the door of my little sanctuary for either treatments, training courses, workshops, or retreats - thank you for choosing me to be by your side. It has been a privilege to witness how meditation, and reiki, have changed your lives and it has been a joy to support you all.

Notes

CHAPTER 2

Changes to the nervous system: Benson, Herbert. *The Relaxation Response.* New York: William Morrow, 1976.

Neuroplasticity and Meditation: 'Buddha's Brain: Neuroplasticity and Meditation' by Richard J Davidson, et al, *National Library of Medicine* PMID: 20871742

Davidson, Richard. 'Meditation and Neuroplasticity: Training Your Brain.' *EXPLORE* 1, no. 5 (2005): 380–88.

'Absence of structural brain changes from mindfulness-based stress reduction: Two combined randomized controlled trials' by Richard J Davidson et al, *National Library of Medicine* PMID: 35594344

Changes to the grey matter of the brain: Lazar, Sara W. 'Meditation Experience Is Associated with Increased Cortical Thickness.' *NeuroReport* 16, no. 17 (2005): 1893–97.

Luders, Eileen. 'The Underlying Anatomical Correlates of Long-Term Meditation: Larger Hippocampal and Frontal Volumes of Gray Matter.' *NeuroImage* 45, no. 3 (2009): 672–78.

Changes to the amygdala: Hölzel, Britta K. et al. 'Stress Reduction Correlates with Structural Changes in the

Amygdala.' *Social Cognitive and Affective Neuroscience* 5, no. 1 (2009): 11–17.

Brain wave changes: Lagopoulos, Jim et al. 'Increased Theta and Alpha Eeg Activity during Nondirective Meditation.' *The Journal of Alternative and Complementary Medicine* 15, no. 11 (2009): 1187–92.

Increase of gamma waves: Lutz, Antoine et al. 'Long-Term Meditators Self-Induce High-Amplitude Gamma Synchrony during Mental Practice.' *Proceedings of the National Academy of Sciences* 101, no. 46 (2004): 16369–73.

CHAPTER 5

Brain wave changes: Hebert, R, and D Lehmann. 'Theta bursts: an EEG pattern in normal subjects practising the transcendental meditation technique.' *Electroencephalography and clinical neurophysiology* vol. 42,3 (1977): 397-405. doi:10.1016/0013-4694(77)90176-6

CHAPTER 6

Gut-brain connection: Cryan, John F et al. 'The Microbiota-Gut-Brain Axis.' *Physiological reviews* vol. 99,4 (2019): 1877-2013.

How stress impacts the immune system: Padgett, David A., and Ronald Glaser. 'How Stress Influences the Immune Response.' *Trends in Immunology* 24, no. 8 (2003): 444–48.

Secondary pain: 'Primary and Secondary Suffering.' NHS Physical Health Psychology Cumbria. NHS. Accessed

February 22, 2023. https://php.cumbria.nhs.uk/patients/resources/ppss-living-well-group/primary-and-secondary-suffering.

Reducing pain activity in the brain: Nakata, Hiroki, Kiwako Sakamoto, and Ryusuke Kakigi. 'Meditation Reduces Pain-Related Neural Activity in the Anterior Cingulate Cortex, Insula, Secondary Somatosensory Cortex, and Thalamus.' *Frontiers in Psychology* 5 (2014).

CHAPTER 7

Guided visualisation description: 'Guided Imagery' *Headspace* https://www.headspace.com/meditation/guided-imagery

Aphantasia: James Gallagher, 'Aphantasia: Ex-Pixar chief Ed Catmull says 'my mind's eye is blind' *BBC News* (2019) https://www.bbc.co.uk/news/health-47830256

How guided visualisations reduce anxiety: Tsitsi, Theologia, Andreas Charalambous, Evridiki Papastavrou, and Vasilios Raftopoulos. 'Effectiveness of a Relaxation Intervention (Progressive Muscle Relaxation and Guided Imagery Techniques) to Reduce Anxiety and Improve Mood of Parents of Hospitalized Children with Malignancies: A Randomized Controlled Trial in Republic of Cyprus and Greece.' *European Journal of Oncology Nursing* 26 (2017): 9–18.

Guided imagery used as anxiety-reducing interventions in breast and prostate cancer: Charalambous, Andreas, Margarita Giannakopoulou, Evangelos Bozas, and Lefkios Paikousis. 'A Randomized Controlled Trial for the

Effectiveness of Progressive Muscle Relaxation and Guided Imagery as Anxiety Reducing Interventions in Breast and Prostate Cancer Patients Undergoing Chemotherapy.' *Evidence-Based Complementary and Alternative Medicine* 2015 (2015): 1–10.

Hamilton, David. *How Your Mind Can Heal Your Body*. Hay House UK; Anniversary Edition, 2018

CHAPTER 8

Salzberg, Sharon. *Real Happiness: A 28-Day Programme To Connect With The Power of Meditation*. Hay House UK, 2020

Williams, Mark & Penman, Danny. *Mindfulness: A Practical Guide to Finding Peace in a Frantic World.* Little, Brown Book Group, 2011

How labelling reduces the brain's emotional centres: Lieberman, Matthew D et al. 'Putting feelings into words: affect labeling disrupts amygdala activity in response to affective stimuli.' *Psychological science* vol. 18,5 (2007): 421-8.

CHAPTER 10

Bernstein, Gabrielle. *Judgement Detox: Release the Beliefs That Hold You Back from Living a Better Life.* Hay House UK, 2018

Hamilton, David. *Why Kindness is Good For You.* Hay House UK, 2010

Loving-kindness increasing positive emotions and decreasing negative emotions: Fredrickson, Barbara L.,

Michael A. Cohn, Kimberly A. Coffey, Jolynn Pek, and Sandra M. Finkel. 'Open Hearts Build Lives: Positive Emotions, Induced through Loving-Kindness Meditation, Build Consequential Personal Resources.' *Journal of Personality and Social Psychology* 95, no. 5 (2008): 1045–62.

How loving-kindness can help with social connections: Kok, Bethany E., Kimberly A. Coffey, Michael A. Cohn, Lahnna I. Catalino, Tanya Vacharkulksemsuk, Sara B. Algoe, Mary Brantley, and Barbara L. Fredrickson. 'How Positive Emotions Build Physical Health.' *Psychological Science* 24, no. 7 (2013): 1123–32.

How loving-kindness can increase empathy: Klimecki, Olga M., Susanne Leiberg, Claus Lamm, and Tania Singer. 'Functional Neural Plasticity and Associated Changes in Positive Affect after Compassion Training.' *Cerebral Cortex* 23, no. 7 (2012): 1552–61.

How loving-kindness can curb your inner critic: Shahar, Ben et al. 'A Wait-List Randomized Controlled Trial of Loving-Kindness Meditation Programme for Self-Criticism.' *Clinical Psychology & Psychotherapy* 22, no. 4 (2014): 346–56.

CHAPTER 11

Neff, Kristen and Germer, Christopher. *The Mindful Self Compassion Workbook: A Proven Way to Accept Yourself, Build Inner Strength, and Thrive.* Guildford Press, 2018

Germer, Christopher. *The Mindful Path to Self-Compassion: Freeing Yourself from Destructive Thoughts and Emotions,* Guildford Press, 2009

Chapter 12

How gratitude can boost happiness: Sheldon, Kennon M., and Sonja Lyubomirsky. 'How to Increase and Sustain Positive Emotion: The Effects of Expressing Gratitude and Visualizing Best Possible Selves.' *The Journal of Positive Psychology* 1, no. 2 (2006): 73–82.

How gratitude can help with perceived stress and mental health: Valikhani, Ahmad, Fatemeh Ahmadnia, Alma Karimi, and Paul J. Mills. 'The Relationship between Dispositional Gratitude and Quality of Life: The Mediating Role of Perceived Stress and Mental Health.' *Personality and Individual Differences* 141 (2019): 40–46.

Gratitude and sleep: Wood, Alex M., Stephen Joseph, Joanna Lloyd, and Samuel Atkins. 'Gratitude Influences Sleep through the Mechanism of Pre-Sleep Cognitions.' *Journal of Psychosomatic Research* 66, no. 1 (2009): 43–48.

Chapter 13

The pain of rejection: 'Social rejection shares somatosensory representations with physical pain' by Ethan Kross, et al, *National Library of Medicine* PMID: 21444827

'The Tale of Two Wolves' *The Nanticoke Indian Tribe,* 2011 *https://www.nanticokeindians.org/page/tale-of-two-wolves*

Printed in Great Britain
by Amazon

23508162R00099